Praise for *Collabo.*

"We've all gotten stuck working with people we don't like. Thankfully, Deb Mashek has written a lively, actionable book to fix that. Combining her expertise as a psychologist and her experience as a consultant, she reveals how we can earn trust, repair relationships, and create collaborations that bring out the best in us."
ADAM GRANT, #1 New York Times bestselling author of
***THINK AGAIN* and host of the TED podcast WorkLife**

"There's so much to love about *Collabor(h)ate*. Too many people are thrown into the deep end of teamwork and left to sink or swim. Sadly, many are sinking. Now we finally have a life buoy. This book is full of new insights about why work relationships are hard and what you can do to make them easier. Better yet, Mashek gives you everything you need to work your team through her brilliant collaboration workshop on your own. This book should be essential reading for every team."
LIANE DAVEY, New York Times best-selling author of
You First* and *The Good Fight

"Cooperation is one of the essential skills in the modern world. *Collabor(h)ate* offers the blueprint for helping people and organizations unlock their potential to work together."
JAY VAN BAVEL, co-author of *The Power of Us*

"Dr. Deb Mashek was born to do this work. She is the relationship psychologist in your pocket, helping you deal with the messy business of people at work. She offers tips, tools, and conversation scripts based on the science of relationships. If you feel like collaborations are happening to you, *Collabor(h)ate* shows you how to shape your decisions, contributions, and outcomes proactively."
TAMMY HEERMANN, author of *Reframe Your Story*

"Whether it's working in teams, or on group projects in the classroom, everyone has a story about a dysfunctional collaboration. In *Collabor(h)ate*, Dr. Deb Mashek shows us how to minimize the stumbling blocks that occur when people work together, but more than that, she provides step-by-step plans for getting the most out of collaborative work. This book will lead you to love collaboration and its many benefits."

RONALD RIGGIO, Henry R. Kravis Professor of Leadership and Organizational Psychology, Claremont McKenna College

"If you're looking for a clear, concise, and action-oriented read on how to improve your collaborations at work, then this book is for you. Deb Mashek grounds her book in practical guidance on how to facilitate better collaborative relationships—while being honest about what makes these relationships hard and unappealing—making this book a how-to-guide you will want to turn to time and time again."

TESSA WEST, author of *Jerks at Work*

"*Collabor(h)ate* teaches what business schools don't: How to build powerful collaborative relationships to unlock the potential of individuals, teams, and organizations. This ultimate guide is a must-read for every executive ready to make collaboration a competitive advantage."

NAOMI BAGDONAS, Lecturer, Stanford's Graduate School of Business, co-author of *Humor, Seriously*

"Collaboration is an essential skill in the workplace and beyond. But it isn't always easy. In *Collabor(h)ate*, social psychologist Deb Mashek demystifies the complex relationships that sit at the heart of collaboration, providing research-informed strategies and tools for realizing the promise and potential of human connection."

SCOTT BARRY KAUFMAN, author of *Transcend* and host of The Psychology Podcast

"I was gripped from the first line. Mashek's the real thing. This book is intensely smart, informed with real science—and enormously useful. We humans evolved to live in collaborative groups. This book shows you how. It's a wise and thought-provoking read."

HELEN FISHER, Chief Science Advisor to Match.com, author of *Anatomy of Love*

"Remote work and social media have made collaborations more difficult and conflict-prone in recent years. It's going to get much worse as Gen Z enters the workforce—a generation that was deprived of opportunities to learn collaboration naturally, in free play. This is why *Collabor(h)ate* is such an important book. Mashek combines psychological research, long experience, and playful writing to show you why collaboration is so vital to organizational and personal success, and how to do it better. This book will make you more valuable to employers, and it will also improve your relationships and well-being as you collaborate with selfish, prickly, egotistical (i.e., normal) human beings."

JON HAIDT, Thomas Cooley Professor of Ethical Leadership, New York University—Stern School of Business, New York Times best-selling author of *The Righteous Mind* and co-author of *The Coddling of the American Mind*

Collabor(h)ate

How to build incredible collaborative
relationships at work
(even if you'd rather work alone)

Deb Mashek, PhD

First published in Great Britain by Practical Inspiration Publishing, 2023

ISBN   9781788603829 (print)
       9781788603843 (epub)
       9781788603836 (mobi)

Illustrations by Amy Trinh (www.atrinhdesign.com).

Author photograph by Belden Carlson (www.beldencarlson.com).

Every effort has been made to trace copyright holders and to obtain their permission for the use of copyright material. The publisher apologizes for any errors or omissions and would be grateful if notified of any corrections that should be incorporated in future reprints or editions of this book.

Want to bulk-buy copies of this book for your team and colleagues? We can introduce case studies, customize the content, and co-brand *Collabor(h)ate* to suit your business's needs.

Please email info@practicalinspiration.com for more details.

Practical Inspiration
Publishing

To Rocco, for being my favorite collaborator and my favorite collaboration.

To Jo Claire, Manon Loustaunau, and Michael Nanfito,

for being the collaborGREAT-est.

To Gerry Ohrstrom, for unlocking serendipity.

Table of Contents

Preface: From trailer park to PhD

THE TRAILER PARK. My parents' alcoholism. My PhD. These were my three great teachers of collaboration.

I spent my childhood in a trailer park in Western Nebraska. Summer days were spent outside, engaged in mixed-age, mixed-gender play. We turned the empty lots into restaurants, the trees into exclusive club houses, and the asphalt grid on which the trailers rested into a play mat for ornate games of hide and seek.

The adults were largely absent; this was, after all, in the 1970s, before milk cartons broadcast missing children and before a culture of parental protectionism took hold. Us kids figured out on our own how to coordinate across interests, to set and enforce rules, and to take care of each other along the way. Free range play meant I had plenty of opportunity to build the social skills that I would later need to be an effective collaborator.

And then there were my parents. Unbeknownst to me at the time (and admittedly perverse), my parents' chronic alcoholism was a second great teacher for collaboration. As with so many kids who grow up amid addiction, home life was chaotic. Adults acted like children. Children acted like adults.

I learned to track and respond to others' needs and to figure out how to smooth over differences of opinion with grace. These interpersonal strategies—childhood superpowers, really—ensured that I could hold onto whatever threads of connection I could find. Often, that connection would come from caring adults outside my family. Teachers, youth group leaders, and parents of friends. I learned to draw positive attention and affection from others by being useful, by being pleasant, and by anticipating needs. Connecting with others meant they would provide what I craved most: security.

As a scrawny kid with huge buck teeth, I figured out how to play nice as if my well-being depended on it because, well, it did. Now, as an adult, I've worked diligently in the therapy room and beyond to turn those default settings into deliberate decisions, choosing when to activate these powers while also recognizing—and voicing—my needs and wants along the way.

Thanks to an incredible high school guidance counselor, I made it to college. With the help of Pell grants,[1] a pile of student loans I acquired with exactly no understanding of what I was signing up for, and a cadre of interested and supportive professors and staff, I thrived in college and found my way to graduate school. There, I discovered the psychology of close relationships.

I found the field fascinating. First, I had no idea a field of study existed in which scholars focused on understanding what makes relationships work. Second, I knew from my very first day in Dr. Arthur Aron's graduate seminar titled *Psychology of Close Relationships* that I wanted to know what those scholars knew. I wanted to know what it takes to create the sort of healthy relationships I found utterly foreign and completely unprepared to pursue or realize.

---

[1] Pell grants are grants offered by the US government to students with exceptional financial need.

So I dug in.

I've spent the past 25 years learning about the psychology of relationships and applying that knowledge to real world challenges like collaboration building.

During that time, I've had the honor of becoming a tenured Full Professor at an elite liberal arts school in the US. Then, worried about the state of polarization in the US and around the world, I walked away from that dream job in 2018, moved cross-country from California to New York as a single mom with an eight-year-old in tow,[2] and helped launch a national nonprofit dedicated to promoting constructive dialogue across lines of difference. Later, I formalized my business of applying relationship science to help people build healthier collaborations and cultures in the workplace.

I'd like to say that I approach collaboration first and foremost as a researcher, but that's not true. I approach collaboration first and foremost as a kid from the trailer park who figured out early on the power of relationships to realize possibilities. The wisdom I gained growing up became the object of my inquiry as a scholar. And that inquiry, in turn, became my lens for helping people who either need or want to work well with others.

I'd like to say that I approach collaboration first and foremost as a researcher, but that's not true. I approach collaboration first and foremost as a kid from the trailer park who figured out early on the power of relationships to realize possibilities.

These habits of heart and mind developed out of necessity as I navigated as gracefully as I could

---

[2] My commitment to collaboration extends deep into my personal life, as well: I didn't even interview for this new opportunity in New York until conferring with my kiddo's dad, from whom I'm divorced, to ask if he'd consider making the move with us, knowing it wouldn't have been healthy for any of us to separate them. He said yes.

the complexities of my early years. I wouldn't change those experiences—and that learning—even if I could. They're the reason that collaboration resides as my core value. They're the reason I am able to help others build incredible collaborations so that they can achieve together what they can't achieve alone.

This brings me neatly to today and to this book.

It was in the fall of 2021. I sat on my couch contemplating whether I should pursue my idea of writing a book about collaboration. Did I have anything original to say about the topic? Would my knowledge be useful to others? My inner voice—that kid from the trailer park—wondered if anyone would care to hear the perspectives of someone like her anyway.

That evening, a sign from the universe landed in my LinkedIn feed: A post by Jay Van Bavel, co-author of *The power of us*,[3] appeared, citing a 2021 *Harvard Business Review* article by Andrea Dittmann, Nichole Stephens, and Sarah Townsend. The authors, discussing their research on how social-class background plays out in workplace teams, noted, "... our work suggests that people from lower social-class backgrounds are likely to bring unique, collaborative skills to organizations that help teams perform well."

That was just the nudge I needed. That evening I decided to share my unique, collaborative skills with others. I decided to write this book.

I am far from a perfect collaborator, no doubt. If you were to ask my collaborators what it's like to work with me, they'd tell you I get ridiculously intense when I get stressed out. While I have a lot of trust in others right from the start, if someone violates that trust, it's inordinately difficult to earn it back. I'm notorious for

---

[3] Van Bavel, J. J., & Packer, D. J. (2021). *The power of us: Harnessing our shared identities to improve performance, increase cooperation, and promote social harmony.* New York, NY: Little, Brown Spark.

adopting new digital to-do lists and project management systems only to revert midstream (and with little warning) to my tried-and-true paper checklists and sticky notes.

While I don't claim to have all the answers or a one-size-fits-all plan for moving us all toward the promised land of collaborGREAT, here's what I can offer:

- I have spent over two decades both studying how people form relationships with each other and applying relationship theory to help people do amazing things together.
- I am an award-winning teacher and have led professional development efforts for faculty at one of our nation's premier institutions.
- I have helped colleges and universities build powerful inter-campus collaborations.
- I have stood in the center of the culture wars and built bridges across ideological divides.
- I have helped business leaders diagnose and address the collaboration headwinds that were tanking their organizations' timelines, bottom lines, and morale.

I love collaboration. I believe it's a skill that can and should be taught. And, I love teaching it.

Whatever your past experiences with collaboration, whether you're more on the side of collabor(h)ate or collaborGREAT, you will find insights in this book that will make visible—and thus navigable—the relationship principles at play in your workplace collaborations. Throughout, I've applied the relationship theory I know to a problem I care about. The result (I hope, for your sake) is an accessible, engaging playbook that illuminates the path through the hidden collaboration curriculum that your—and your organization's—success depends on.

Perhaps it won't come as a surprise that a book about collaboration highlights the ideas of others alongside my own, including:

- The multitude of scholars whose work has informed my thinking over the years about how to make relationships work; the research I've been reading, teaching, and contributing to for over two decades yielded the insights and concrete tools presented here.

- Over 50 individuals who sat down with me for formal interviews and informal conversations about collaboration in their worlds—CEOs, journalists, a firefighter, a nurse, venture capitalists, technologists, entrepreneurs, project managers, founders, HR experts, nonprofit leaders, miners, architects, teachers, wranglers, and philanthropists.

- My clients whose journeys through the trials and tribulations of collaboration continue to reveal lessons.

- Hundreds of people who have engaged my thinking with generosity and care on LinkedIn, Facebook, and even TikTok.

- 1,100 people who shared their experiences and wisdom in the Workplace Collaboration Survey (see Appendix A for an overview).

I weave their stories, quotes, and data throughout the book to hit home the promise and peril of collaboration. Written for professionals whose livelihood depends on their ability to work well with others, this book is shaped as follows.

Chapter 1 invites readers to take a step back from the full-throated celebration of collaboration that's often present in many workplaces, instead acknowledging that collaboration can be really difficult to do well and that it is often fraught with disappointment, frustration, and worse. This chapter gives voice to the silent H tucked away in the book's title, making the case that we must first acknowledge this pain if we have any hope of creating collaborative relationships that are healthy, effective, and sustainable.

Chapter 2 introduces the Mashek Matrix as a simple model for thinking about what differentiates relationships that are collaborGREAT from those that are collabor(h)ate. Built on the two dimensions of relationship quality and interdependence, this model offers a counterintuitive path for improving collaborative relationships.

Chapter 3 and Chapter 4, in turn, draw on empirical research in the psychology of close relationships to offer strategies for deliberately moving one's relationship along the path from collabor(h)ate to collaborGREAT. Chapter 3 focuses on relationship quality, while Chapter 4 tackles interdependence.

Chapter 5 offers a step-by-step approach for leveraging the Mashek Matrix to improve your collaborations.

With eyes wide open and in full recognition that collaborations don't always live up to the hype, Chapter 6 takes a brutally honest look at when and how to end collaborative relationships.

Chapter 7 considers what your life may look like as you hone your approach and effectiveness as an extraordinary collaborator. Knowing you'll be on others' radar as someone who plays well with others, how will you decide which opportunities to say yes to? And how will you identify other incredible collaborators with whom to work? Given the critical role collaboration plays in our friendships, family, community, and life beyond work, the chapter ends by considering how principles from the book apply to those important domains.

Along the way, a couple repeating elements will support both your reading experience and your ability to pull key ideas forward into the real world. These are:

Toolboxes contain takeaway tools that either augment or encapsulate ideas from the main text.

Digital downloads are ancillary materials you may want to engage as you read the book; these are signaled throughout the book with a download icon.

Here's the point sections, which appear at the end of each chapter, summarize that chapter's key ideas.

Take 5 sections contain coaching questions—five to be exact—that encourage you to reflect on how the ideas from the chapter connect to your beliefs, experiences, or aspirations. Spend five minutes at the end of each chapter to ponder these questions; doing so will increase the likelihood you will carry forward key ideas into your daily life.

Collaboration has existed as a tool for doing since the beginning of humankind. Providing for the necessities of food and shelter were communal affairs on the rugged savannahs of our ancestors. In much more recent history, those barns didn't raise themselves.

In our modern world, collaboration holds the key to solving the world's most complex problems. For both individuals and organizations, collaboration is—ironically—a competitive advantage, unlocking potential and driving progress.

> *For both individuals and organizations, collaboration is—ironically—a competitive advantage, unlocking potential and driving progress.*

But, just because collaboration is familiar, longstanding, and crucial, it doesn't mean it is easy to do well. As my then-12-year-old quipped one night before tucking in, "Working together is super easy, said no one ever."

Let's make a dent in that shared challenge, shall we?

Chapter 1

What is collaboration and how does it go sideways?

What is "collaboration" anyway?

MANY PEOPLE MOVE about the world with a vague sense that working together is a good thing—something we *should* do. Individuals strive to collaborate in their relationships, work lives, and extracurriculars. Companies big and small proclaim collaboration a core value. A tennis shoe company teams up with a bag of potato chips to save the environment. Put a couple smart people with good ideas on a project, the thinking goes, and you'll get lightning.

But what is collaboration exactly?

I want to be careful here to not slice and dice the term to become unrecognizable to myself or others; I realize this is a real risk as a recovering academic. Whatever definition I propose needs to feel familiar and meaningful, while also offering some boundaries to clarify what's "in" and what's "out" of the collaboration bucket.

The parts of the word itself say a lot about what the word means. "Co-labor" literally means "together work" and the suffix "-ion" points to an act or a process. Collaboration, then, is the process of working together.

That's a good start, but more specificity is needed.

First, the work must be intentional. The individuals who are working toward the shared goal must coordinate or orchestrate that work in some way. Being passionate about the same cause, but working toward that cause independently, does not make two people collaborators just as two toddlers building block towers next to each other in parallel play are not collaborating to create a city.

Second, collaborations exist among known individuals. You can pinpoint specifically who is involved in the collaboration and who isn't. You know their names. It is theoretically possible to gather these folk around a table—or on a Zoom screen—to look eye to eye. Granted, sometimes collaborative groups are too large to truly fit around the table, but even then the individuals on the coordinating team know each other and the people on each sub-team know each other. A diffuse conglomerate of loosely associated individuals isn't a collaboration. (I'm looking at you, democracy.)

Third, the together work must be in service to a specific shared goal. "Make the world a better place," while an admirable recipient of one's energy, does not suffice as a rallying cry for collaboration

Collaboration is the process of two or more known individuals working together intentionally to advance a specific shared goal.

because it lacks specificity. Without specificity, the individuals involved are unable to determine if and when they accomplish the shared goal.

So, all that said, here's the definition of collaboration I'll be using in this book: collaboration is the process of two or more known individuals working together intentionally to advance a specific shared goal.

This definition applies to a wide range of contexts and circumstances. For example, it works for collaborations that are wholly voluntary, as well as those that are "voluntold".[4] It applies to collaborations that exist for a short period of time as well as those that persist for years on end. The definition works just as well for situations where the partners have equal access to resources, status, and power as when those things are wildly asymmetrical. It works just as well for collaborations that are informal as those that are highly structured by contracts and other written agreements. It works just as well for synchronous and asynchronous collaborations. And, it works just as well for in-person, remote, and hybrid collaborations.

You might have other definitional ideas.[5] Check the ideas throughout the book against your definition to see what feels useful. You are, of course, welcome to leverage whatever tools and insights you find valuable and jettison the others.

---

[4] *Voluntold* is a portmanteau that blends "volunteer" and "told." If someone has been voluntold to collaborate, the collaboration has been forced upon them in some way. Perhaps they're not excited for the project or don't see the point of the work. Yet, they have no option not to collaborate.

[5] For one excellent complementary conceptualization of collaboration, check out Arthur Himmelman's Collaboration Continuum, which states that collaboration lies on a continuum of different forms of working together that ranges from networking (exchanging information for mutual benefit), to coordinating (altering activities to achieve a common purpose), to cooperating (sharing resources), to collaborating (learning from each other to enhance each other's capacity). I have summarized Himmelman's continuum, and articulated the capacities and supports needed to enact each station well, in a handout available in the Other Links section of www.collaborhate.com.

How common is collaboration in the workplace?

Based on this definition, I asked 1,100 participants in the Workplace Collaboration Survey what proportion of their job entails collaborating with others to advance shared goals. Keep in mind that, to be included in the sample in the first place, participants had to report that they work with others at least sometimes, which means lone rangers[6] were not included in the study. With that caveat aside, the results are striking:

- 12% collaborate between 1–20% of the time.
- 16% collaborate between 21–40% of the time.
- 24% collaborate between 41–60% of the time.
- 25% collaborate between 61–80% of the time.
- 22% collaborate over 81% of the time.

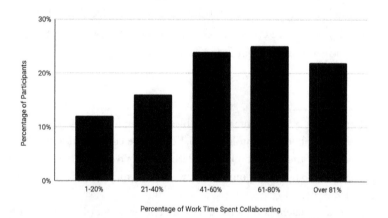

WHAT PROPORTION OF YOUR JOB ENTAILS COLLABORATING
WITH OTHERS TO ADVANCE SHARED GOALS?

---

[6] Of the 5,372 Prolific respondents who otherwise met all inclusion criteria for the Workplace Collaboration Survey, 457 (8.5%) answered "No" to Prolific's screening item, "Does your work require you to regularly interact with other employees (e.g., co-workers, colleagues, subordinates, assistants)?"

In other words, 71% of the sample reported spending at least 41% of their work life—that's over three hours per day in a "typical" work day—collaborating with others. (When asked how much time they would *ideally* spend collaborating, 47% expressed an eagerness to spend at least 41% of their time collaborating.)

People tended to have between two to five collaborations generally involving three to seven collaborators.[7] On average, people reported being involved in just under six collaborations. These collaborations on average involved just under six core collaborators.

There's no shortage of collaboration out there. Why is that? Why do so many of us invest time, energy, and other resources in collaboration?

Why is collaboration so common?

Workplace collaboration is common for at least three reasons.

First, I'll start with the least interesting reason: In many organizations, people create goods, products, and services within an incredibly complex web of relationships, interests, resources, policies, workflows, and information. Because no one person can know or do everything, collaboration among individuals, departments, divisions, and even organizations is necessary to bring even relatively basic ideas to fruition.

As one example, imagine an in-house trainer wishes to hire an external speaker to deliver a workshop. Someone in Accounts Payable gets involved to pay the invoice. Someone in Communications

---

[7] Of the sample, 10% reported having 9 or more collaborations with 6 people reporting 100 collaborations. And, 10% of the sample reported generally having a large number of collaborators, ranging from 11 to 12,000. Gulp. Due to the anonymized nature of the survey, I was unable to reach out to ask clarifying follow-up questions.

gets involved to design the promotional materials. Someone in IT gets involved to ensure the off-site visitor has the required credentials to launch the presentation. Someone in Facilities may take lead on room setup. Granted, some organizations are unnecessarily ornate in their structure, but the point remains: collaboration is often required simply to navigate through the complexity of the workplace itself.

Second, and much more interesting, collaboration enables solutions to complex problems by bringing together disparate skill sets, expertises, perspectives, and resources. While working alone is limiting in that we are constrained to use only those tools and capacities that we either already have or could somehow acquire, working with others magnifies those resources. It's like the carpenter, the electrician, the plumber, the landscaper, and the finisher all open their toolboxes to each other and say, hey, between the lot of us, we've got what we need to build a house. Or an office building. Or a skyscraper. Let's get to work.

A scientist I interviewed observed that the scope of the questions being asked in many fields, the varied arenas of knowledge that must be integrated to answer them, and the availability of new technologies to explore them mean that "science now requires a level of collaboration that has never happened before."

Third, collaboration can drive innovation. Cross-functional, skip-rank, interorganizational, intergenerational, and cross-cultural collaborations offer especially rich opportunities for transformative collaborations precisely because they bring together broad perspectives and talents, afford more novelty and thus self-expansion, and bubble up more compelling solutions. Cool stuff happens when diverse people from diverse backgrounds with diverse talents advance diverse interests within the context of collaboration.

A 2014 study published in *Nature*, for example, found that scientific papers co-authored by ethnically diverse teams "make more of a splash in the scientific literature."[8] Compared to papers by ethnically homogenous co-authors, papers authored by diverse teams appear in more prestigious journals and are cited more often by others.

More generally, evidence drawn from finance, business, management, board composition, and law suggests demographically diverse teams make smarter decisions and generate more innovative thinking.[9] As David Rock and Heidi Grant summarize in their *Harvard Business Review* article on the topic, "... enriching your employee pool with representatives of different genders, races, and nationalities is key for boosting your company's joint intellectual potential. Creating a more diverse workplace will help to keep your team members' biases in check and make them question their assumptions." Diversity, in addition to being a valued goal in its own right, is also then a means to an end: it increases the perspectives available to solve complex problems. Antonin Scalia, a conservative justice on the US Supreme court, knew this well, which is why he reportedly always took on at least one left-leaning clerk to balance out his conservative bias.[10]

All told, collaboration is common because it makes the impossible possible. It is essential to address the big challenges we face in business, civics, education, and beyond. Collaboration is a competitive advantage. Or, rather, *good* collaboration is a competitive advantage.

---

[8] Freeman, R., & Huang, W. (2014). Collaboration: Strength in diversity. *Nature, 513*, 305. https://doi.org/10.1038/513305a

[9] Rock, D., & Grant, H. (2016, November 4). *Why diverse teams are smarter. Harvard Business Review.* Retrieved August 8, 2022 from www.hbr.org/2016/11/why-diverse-teams-are-smarter

[10] *The Guardian.* (2016, February 15). Antonin Scalia: Liberal clerks reflect on the man they knew and admired. Retrieved August 8, 2022 from www.theguardian.com/law/2016/feb/15/antonin-scalia-supreme-court-justice-liberal-clerks-reflect

What's at stake when collaboration sizzles versus fizzles?

What is at stake when collaboration sizzles versus fizzles? I asked this question of the people I interviewed for the book and of colleagues online. Here are the themes that emerged about the benefits of collaboration.

You benefit when collaboration sizzles:

- You acquire new abilities, resources, and perspectives.
- Your network expands and you deepen relationships.
- Professional opportunities become available to you.
- Your reputation receives a boost.
- You have more fun at work.

Teams benefit when collaboration sizzles:

- Individuals feel more engaged with their work.
- They feel visible and valued.
- The value created by the team is maximized.
- The team gains quicker access to decentralized information and quicker feedback.

Projects benefit when collaboration sizzles:

- The team's work is enhanced by viewpoint diversity, resulting in stronger ideas and better solutions.
- More creative thinking is evidenced.
- Competing priorities are optimized.
- Customers and clients have a more positive experience.

And, *organizations* benefit when collaboration sizzles:

- Skills and resources are more effectively deployed.
- Efficiencies are realized.
- Bottom lines are bolstered.
- Great programs and services are implemented and consistently executed.

- Talent is retained.
- Larger returns on investment are realized.
- Organization becomes known as a place with a good collaborative culture.

As the themes above make clear, collaboration can bring with it incredible benefits. However, when done poorly, collaboration is a huge sink of time, money, and human potential. Here's what's at stake when collaboration fizzles.

You suffer when collaboration fizzles:

- Your stress and frustration levels increase.
- You carry these stresses home with you.
- Your reputation takes a hit.
- You are less able to bring your unique gifts to your work.
- You experience lower job satisfaction and morale.

Teams suffer when collaboration fizzles:

- Suspicion and distrust emerge.
- Teams feel less confident in their work.
- They exhibit lower productivity.
- Teams miss out on new and creative ideas that are sparked by others' perspectives.
- Bad collaborators become more isolated.

Projects suffer when collaboration fizzles:

- Project budgets and timelines get busted.
- Weaker solutions and products emerge.
- Customer pain points are not addressed.

And, *organizations* suffer when collaboration fizzles:

- Invisible headwinds decrease efficiency and effectiveness.
- Morale tanks.
- Talent turns over, triggering direct and indirect rehiring costs.

- Time, talent, and treasure are wasted.
- Clients walk.

In sum, poor collaboration is an incredible liability. When collaboration goes wrong, everything is at stake. As one business leader said, "It follows you around like a cart full of bricks."

Mixed feelings about collaboration? Welcome to the club

Given the incredible range of outcomes associated with collaborations that sizzle versus fizzle, it's no surprise that a lot of people hold mixed feelings about collaboration.

What about you? What three words or phrases best describe your thoughts and feelings about workplace collaboration?

I ask this same question at the beginning of my collaboration workshops, on social media to generate interesting discussion, of individuals when they apply to join my online community, of strangers who ask what I do for a living, and—you guessed it—of participants in my research.

Many people share a mix of positive and negative words and phrases. Alongside positive descriptors such as "opportunity," "success," "essential," and "potential," people share negative descriptors like "scary," "risky," "apprehension," and "painful."

Self-report data from varied samples echo this mixed sentiment.

In Spring 2021, I teamed up with College Pulse,[11] an online survey and analytics company, to ask a representative sample of 500 current college students their opinions on team-based class projects.

---

[11] www.collegepulse.com [Accessed July 11, 2022].

The data, originally published by *The Hechinger Report*,[12] showed that nearly half (49%) of the students characterized their feelings about team-based class projects as either "somewhat negative" or "very negative"; only 2% felt "very positive."

Participants in the Workplace Collaboration Survey held more positive views toward collaboration. The average response on a 7-point scale, where higher numbers reflected more positive attitudes toward collaboration, was 5.29.

Yet, even within this generally positive sample, 72% reported having been in at least one collaboration that was "absolutely horrendous." Thankfully, 85% reported having been in at least one that was "absolutely incredible." This means, of course, that most people (63%, in fact) have experienced both the highs and the lows of workplace collaboration.

Participants in the Workplace Collaboration Survey also felt ambivalent about the people with whom they collaborate. When asked to rate their collaborative relationship on a visual analog scale that corresponded with values from 0 to 100, where 0 equaled "CollaborHATE" and 100 equaled "CollaborGREAT," respondents used the full range of the scale.

In other words, a whole lot of people out there have mixed feelings about collaboration. They know it is ripe with potential and that it can be incredibly rewarding. *And* they know it can also be an incredible burden, ripe with headache and heartache.

If you likewise have ambivalent feelings about collaboration, welcome to the club.

---

[12] Mashek, D. (2021, June 23). College graduates lack preparation in the skill most valued by employers—collaboration. *The Hechinger Report*. Retrieved August 8, 2022 from www.hechingerreport.org/opinion-college-graduates-lack-preparation-in-the-skill-most-valued-by-employers-collaboration/

Let's talk about the silent H in collabor(h)ate

Despite all the mixed feelings, many people *want* to collaborate. And, they want to be *good* collaborators.

Perhaps they value the spirit of collaboration. Or it's something they believe will advance their personal or professional goals. Or they know in their bones that their ability to change the world will be unlocked only in partnership with others. Or maybe it's something they want their teams to do well, but, when they actually attempt to model collaboration, they release a Pandora's Box of messiness, complication, and frustration.

Culturally, there are a whole lot of messages flying around about how collaboration is some combination of bees' knees, sliced bread, the end-all-be-all, and the right solution for every challenge. Yet, as all the mixed feelings point to, collaboration can really, really suck.

I want us to talk about that struggle. I want it to be acceptable to say out loud, "Argh, this whole playing well with others thing is really difficult." I want to give permission to everyone who is skeptical of the rah-rah collaboration messages out there to say, "Hold up. I see it differently. Let's take a real look at what's not working here so we can figure out how to do it better."

Let's give voice to the H in Collabor(h)ate. Silencing it means missing out on critical opportunities to learn what we and our colleagues are struggling with, thus obscuring pathways to making this whole working together thing way more positive for way more people. Understanding the interpersonal dynamics at play, and designing our collaborations accordingly, means we can make collaborations more productive, sustainable, enjoyable, and healthy.

Collaboration, why do I hate thee? Let me count the ways

As a first step in giving voice to the H in collabor(h)ate, here are 24 (yes, 24!) of the common ways collaborations go sideways. Buckle up.

Dropped balls. Someone says they will do something, but then they either don't do it or they do something that doesn't align with what others were expecting them to do. Or, perhaps the meeting invite or important email thread left off (intentionally or not) someone who needs to be in the loop. As one CEO said when I asked what goes wrong in collaborations: "Some people just don't do their sh*t."

Uneven workload. Whether a function of interests, energy, capacity, or know-how, the work is distributed unevenly—and often unfairly—across the members of the team. Some people end up feeling way under benefited while others end up being total free-riders.

"My way or the highway." Somebody ends up throwing their weight around as the decider, acting on behalf of the full group, perhaps with little or no sincere effort to understand the needs, interests, and preferences of others. Other people end up feeling dragged along.

"I'll just do it myself." An eager collaborator feels as though they alone care enough about the project to do it the "right" way or as quickly as it needs to get done. They may think they're doing everyone else a favor. Or, as suggested by one start-up founder, perhaps they truly feel others are incompetent: "I'm bad at working with people because sometimes they're stupid. And I just ignore them. And then I just do my thing. And I get away with it because the product ends up being really good. I'm not going to wait for a mediocre product from this dumbass who doesn't understand what I'm asking for." One investment fund manager

I spoke with observed, "These individuals are prepared to put the world on their shoulders and carry the project forward. But they have to understand that the answer they come up with on their own is not nearly as rich as if the work had incorporated the views, perspectives, and work from everyone who was part of that collaboration."

No capacity to give. Somebody enthusiastically volunteers to take care of a set of tasks, despite the fact they have no time to actually do those things amid their other commitments. The result? The project backs up, to-dos remain undone, and other people have to rearrange their work to release the log jam—all the while, the person continues to claim they'll get to it. They often apologize profusely, then may try to remedy the situation by spending a few distracted minutes on the project as they jam through their overly packed day.

Under preparation. Due to time pressures, disinterest, or lack of accountability, people arrive to meetings unprepared to fully engage in the shared work at hand. They haven't read the prework or completed the background research they had promised, compromising the team's ability to move the project forward.

Disengagement. Some people don't reply to emails for days. They may attend meetings, but text on their phone the whole time. Whatever the reason, the group doesn't benefit from this person's insights and expertise and they have to waste time downstream revisiting—sometimes, at great expense—issues that have already been covered.

Herding cats. Even with a lot of upfront effort to set goals and expectations, one person shoots off on their own, creating fires for others, not to mention downstream chaos and confusion.

Too-late contributions. Despite an agreed-upon timeline that clearly indicates when input needs to be received, someone withholds their feedback until well past the deadline. When that person finally gets around to giving comments, their feedback, even if it is wonderful and spot-on, causes an avoidable crush of both effort and morale, impacting the work of those both earlier and later in the workflow.

Inconsistent contributions. A collaborator binges on the project one week, and then falls off the face of the earth the next, resurfacing again a week later. Up and down. Back and forth. It becomes impossible to predict and thus plan around their contributions. As one nonprofit leader noted, "I need to know that your past behavior predicts your future behavior. Don't get lazy with our relationship. Work as hard on this contract as you did on the first one. You can't just rest on your laurels."

Stealing credit and placing blame. One person takes credit for others' work or for the team's successes, perhaps while also shirking any responsibility for the failures or placing all the blame for the failures squarely on others' shoulders.

Off-loading risk. Related to stealing credit and placing blame, off-loading risk may pop up in collaborations guided by formal written agreements. In adversarial contracting, the goal is to snag as many of the rewards for oneself as possible while strapping the other party with as many of the risks as possible. A consultant I know won't do business with clients who put lopsided contracts in front of her, protecting their interests (e.g., intellectual property, release of liability), but either squishing or not bothering to mention her interests (e.g., "Hey, I'd like to keep my IP and not get sued, too!").

Egos, titles, and credentials. Someone may be utterly unable or unwilling to go beyond their needs and interests to even consider, much less value, others' needs and interests. The mere fact of their title or letters behind their name may give them the mistaken belief that they alone are capable of making valuable contributions to the cause.

Hoarding and withholding. Even when the collaboration is ostensibly designed with resource sharing in mind, a collaborator hoards access to information, tools, perspectives, or people. Whether due to insecurity, carelessness, an inability or unwillingness to anticipate collaborators' needs, or the absence of clear channels for sharing, hoarding creates unnecessary barriers to completing the work. As one example, an engineer at a multinational tech firm blindsided a project manager on the same team with a slide deck enumerating 14 unmitigated risks he had noticed—and should have shared much earlier—during their months and months of working together.

Tyranny of perfectionism. When someone feels their worth is contingent on presenting only perfect work, they sometimes keep collaborators at arm's length when developing work. Rather than seeking and getting constructive input on half-baked work early in its development, they wait until their piece is as perfect as possible before sharing it, making it difficult for others to contribute and creating a high-stakes environment where feedback can set back timelines or set off emotions.

Dodging hard conversations. Despite the importance of constructive tension in helping teams identify the best path forward, a conflict-averse member of the team may sweep differences of opinions aside, making it difficult for the team to optimize across competing demands. Such behaviors can make it impossible to talk about important issues.

Mushy roles. Poorly defined roles result in confusion, redundant effort, absent talents, and incomplete coverage.

Failing to decide how to decide. Nobody can really explain how decisions are made, resulting in varied expectations and inevitably hurt feelings when people later feel cut out from decision making or burdened by decisions they'd rather not make.

Tool overload. Collaborators mindlessly import their favorite technology tools from other projects into this project without considering the preferences or capabilities of others. Perhaps they heard about new tools to help with communication, task management, or decision archiving and adopt them by fiat. Before you know it, confusion and drag emerge as people try to figure out how to work across disparate tools, struggle to find time to learn a new tool, and are unable to find where key documents and decisions are housed. As one tech consultant shared, "I don't want to adopt another damn tool. Are you kidding me?" A start-up leader echoed, "We are losing productivity because we are consumed by productivity tools."

Asymmetrical power. Whether a function of rank, role, budget, or any number of other personal or situational variables that imbue power within your context, asymmetrical access to power among collaborators can impede information flow, derail due consideration of competing ideas, and hijack the frankness of accountability conversations.

Responsibility without authority. This one is less an issue of someone making a misstep as it is just a reality of the modern workplace. As one tech executive who came up through project management observed, "You've got lots of responsibility and zero authority. The engineers don't work for you, they work for the VP of engineering. They could tell you to go to hell. And yet you're held accountable for the product."

Hiding. Failure to communicate to one's team when you're stuck leaves them to operate under the assumption that all is well and leaves them unable to help clear the path. The tech executive mentioned above said, "You don't want to be dependent on that magic guy in the backroom who's doing a super important thing. Inevitably, he hits a wall and has problems. And now he's scared to tell you and the whole project is going to blow up."

Poisoned well. Sometimes, the culture in an organization or even on a specific team gets so toxic that all trust, goodwill, and care are gone. The proverbial well is poisoned, making it impossible to regain the very assets that enable collaboration. The icky residue of past wrongs builds up, making it impossible to build a climate of trust. As one journalist aptly put it, "Forget collaboration at that point."

Undermining. Undermining is defined as someone intentionally sabotaging a colleague's work over time such that that person's relationships, reputation, or accomplishments take a hit.[13] Spreading rumors and "accidentally" forgetting to bring the handouts to the meeting are both examples of undermining. It's one thing to have to deal with a collaborator who consistently undermines you, but, research suggests that it's even more demoralizing to have to deal with a colleague who is sometimes undermining and sometimes supportive.[14]

Gulp. That's a long list of ways collaboration can go off the rails. Are you also feeling that working on a deserted island doesn't sound like a horrible idea? Frankly, these potholes along the road to collaboration aren't all that surprising given how few people ever receive any training in how to collaborate well.

Do we teach this stuff?

Given collaboration is both difficult and essential, surely we make it a priority to teach people how to do it well, right?

Nope.

Let's first look at college. When I teamed up with College Pulse to survey 500 current college students in the US, we asked how many major group projects the students had been assigned in that one semester. Of the respondents, 35% had been assigned three or more such projects.

---

[13] Duffy, M. K., Ganster, D. C., & Pagon, M. (2002). Social undermining in the workplace. *Academy of Management Journal, 45*(2), 331–351. https://doi-org.ccl.idm.oclc.org/10.2307/3069350

[14] (Duffy et al., 2002)

How much training, if any, had their college provided for ways to make these team-based projects more effective, enjoyable, or productive? Desperately little.

A staggering 65% of respondents said they had received no training. Another 22% said they had received "A few minutes" of training.

Gulp. This means that a whopping 87% of college students lack training in a skill that, according to a study conducted by the Association of American Colleges and Universities, is highly valued by 93% of employers.[15] These findings resonate with a 2017 survey conducted by the Society of Human Resource Management (SHRM) in which 80% of HR professionals reported that job applicants fell short on soft skills.[16] Teamwork and collaboration specifically were cited by 30% of these HR professionals as the reason they were having difficulty recruiting talent.

What about beyond college? MBA programs, for example, are notorious for requiring a lot of group-based assignments from students. Perhaps collaboration skills are taught in business school?

Nope.

One business school professor observed, "We throw them into groups and tell them to work together, but we don't actually give them any tools for how to do that."

---

[15] Finley, A. (2021). *How college contributes to workforce success: Employer views on what matters most.* Association of American Colleges and Universities. Retrieved August 8, 2022 from https://dgmg81phhvh63.cloudfront.net/content/user-photos/Research/PDFs/AACUEmployerReport2021.pdf

[16] Society for Human Resource Management. (2016, June 21). The new talent landscape: Recruiting difficulty and skills shortages. Retrieved August 8, 2022 from www.shrm.org/hr-today/trends-and-forecasting/research-and-surveys/documents/shrm%20new%20talent%20landscape%20recruiting%20difficulty%20skills.pdf

With no training, some people figure out a very light version of working together. The strategy: divide and conquer. The case study has five sections? We'll each take charge of one, get the info we need for our part, and then present. Not surprisingly, the result is often a disjointed mess that lacks the sort of integration and coherence an audience would actually find useful.

As the business school professor noted, "Even if everybody in the group is well motivated and really wants to contribute to the project, I don't think they have any idea how to work together beyond divide and conquer. And you have limited time, so they probably figured that's going to save the most time anyway. But the truth is very little of it is actually collaboration. Most of it is just a semi-coordinated team doing modular functions." He adds, "I actually don't tell them how to do it either. I just say, you know, you're adults. Just do it."

OK, so what about in the workplace? Perhaps we wait until people enter the workforce before investing in their development as collaborators?

Nope.

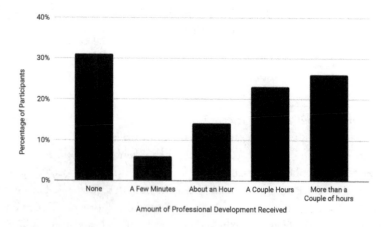

HOW MUCH PROFESSIONAL DEVELOPMENT, IF ANY, HAVE YOU
RECEIVED ON HOW TO BUILD HEALTHY AND PRODUCTIVE
COLLABORATIVE RELATIONSHIPS AT WORK?

Of those in the Workplace Collaboration Survey, 31% said they had received exactly no professional development in how to build healthy and productive collaborative relationships at work. Another 6% said they had received "a few minutes." "About an hour" came from 14%, 23% said "a couple hours," and 26% said "more than a couple hours." In other words, only roughly a quarter of people report receiving anything approximating substantial training in this critical workplace skill.

Here's the most fascinating thing about these data on professional development: There's a consistent positive (and statistically significant) relationship between how much professional development people have received in how to collaborate well and their job satisfaction, their attitudes toward collaboration, and how much time they would ideally spend collaborating with others. While the correlational nature of these data makes it impossible to determine what exactly causes these associations, increased professional development on how to collaborate may actually drive satisfaction, attitudes, and interests.

What kind of professional development are they getting? Keeping in mind that any one person could experience many different forms of professional development, here's what the survey shows:

- 56% received on-the-job training.
- 30% received mentorship.
- 25% attended lectures.
- 25% received coaching.
- 25% took courses or workshops.
- 23% read books.
- 8% indicated "Other."[17]

It's possible that the reason people aren't receiving any training is because they're not interested in receiving training. The data don't

---

[17] In retrospect, I wish I had asked whether people count watching reruns of *The Office* as professional development.

support that conclusion. In fact, when I asked the study participants whether they agreed or disagreed with the statement, "I am
very interested in developing my collaboration skills," 77% agreed.

They're interested in developing their collaboration skills because
they know their professional success depends on their ability to collaborate well. I asked respondents in the Workplace
Collaboration Survey to what extent they agreed or disagreed
with the statement, "My professional success depends on my ability to collaborate well"—81% agreed with this statement. People
get that this stuff is important.

These data and anecdotes leave me dispirited. Think about it:
Collaboration is critically important. It's hard to do well, and yet
there seems to be a general belief that this is a skill one can just
pick up by osmosis via on-the-job training amid a bunch of other
professionals who likewise haven't had any formal training. Like
trying to construct an IKEA dresser without the instructions,
everyone is feeling their way through the muck. It's no wonder
so many collaborative projects encounter snags, fall flat, or result
in good talent heading for the door. We can do better, but where
shall we start?

Where to start?

In addition to being a master collaborator who made his living helping people work together to do more with less, Michael Nanfito
happens to be a builder of boats. I once asked him what we know
about collaboration from the vantage point of boat building.

He observed that boats are aggregates of systems, with different
teams of people involved both in creating each system and in
ensuring the systems work harmoniously. As experts, these individuals have incredible skills; they are passionate about both what
they do and how they do it. Each has tools of their trade at the
ready, knowing when and how to deploy them.

Michael points here to the trifecta on which all collaborations are built: people, tools, and processes.[18] These assets are interrelated, mutually limiting, and mutually amplifying.

If you have poor materials to work with, what you can do with those materials is necessarily constrained. Yet, the materials themselves are not going to make the boat. You must also have the right tools and the right team. Likewise, an incredibly skilled team can do amazing things with mediocre tools and materials, but when you have all three—amazing people, tools, and processes— lightning strikes. As Michael said, "You can do something really well if you have all the right tools and have developed really good processes, you can work with your people to do really wonderful things."

So, yes, all three are important. And, yet, I have chosen to focus this book on the people—in particular, on the relationships among the people. Why?

While surely biased by my expertise in the psychology of close relationships, I humbly assert that healthy collaborative relationships are the first principle of powerful collaborations. No matter the type, quality, or volume of tools and processes, the relationships among the people form the core of any collaboration.

As one nonprofit founder noted, "Good people figure out how to get it done with the tools available to them, even if the tools are crappy... they find a way to get it done."

A vice president of a Fortune 500 company agrees. "Good people can overcome a mediocre process, or even ineffective tools," he said. "If you have a good team, you're going to find a way to get

---

[18] While this book focuses on collaborative relationships, those who are interested in learning about collaborative tools and processes are encouraged to check out my and Michael's 20-page collaboration guide. It is available at www.debmashek.com [Accessed July 11, 2022].

done what needs to get done. If you've got the right team, you can figure out anything."

Some organizational leaders understand that they need to do more ground setting than merely proclaiming, "Go forth and collaborate!" They may invest in collaborative tools, provide release time for individual contributors to learn how to use those tools, and even hire project managers who masterfully coordinate processes. Yet, as one tech consultant shared, "There are people who are trained to project manage the crap out of the logistical parts and the technical parts. But the people parts? Not at all."

And, let's be honest, those people parts are really hard. Relationships are hard. This is a leading reason collaborations are hard. One philanthropy and nonprofit leader observed, "Anything that would be a problem in any other kind of relationship will be a problem in a workplace setting; anything that will throw off a relationship will throw off a collaboration." Bingo.

> *There are people who are trained to project manage the crap out of the logistical parts and the technical parts. But the people parts? Not at all.*

The health of your collaborative relationships makes or breaks not just the outcome of the collaboration itself, but also the positivity (or negativity) of your experience within a collaboration. For this reason, I take a decidedly relationships focus throughout this book.

Fear not, this is learnable

Just as very few of us ever receive any formal training in how to be an incredible spouse, or parent, or friend, as highlighted above, few of us ever receive any coaching in how to be incredible collaborators. Despite the complexity of social relationships, pretty much across the board we're rather expected to either know how to do them or to figure them out as we go along. Sink or swim.

> *Just as very few of us ever receive any formal training in how to be an incredible spouse, or parent, or friend, few of us ever receive any coaching in how to be incredible collaborators.*

That's hardly a strategy to rely on when everything from our emotional well-being, to our joy at work, to our organization's bottom line is at stake. We can do better.

Thank goodness, this relationship stuff is learnable. Like all relationships, collaboration takes work. And, like all relationships, there are better and worse things to do if you want that relationship to thrive.

Close relationships expert Arthur Aron (father of the 36 questions to create closeness[19] and my PhD advisor), shared the following story. Imagine two people decide to open a bakery together. They come up with a great name for their store. They buy all the fanciest tools and the best ingredients. They decide which treats will fill their shelves. And they hang a stunning sign outside their store to proclaim they are open for business.

But that's where the effort stops. They don't hire a skilled baker. They don't advertise. They don't get feedback from their customers. They don't introduce themselves to other business owners in the neighborhood.

---

[19] Aron, A., Melinat, E., Aron, E. N., Vallone, R. D., & Bator, R. J. (1997). The experimental generation of interpersonal closeness: A procedure and some preliminary findings. *Personality and Social Psychology Bulletin, 23*(4), 363–377. https://doi.org/10.1177/0146167297234003. The 36 questions were popularized by a viral article by Mandy Len Catron; Catron, M. L. (2015, January 9). *To fall in love with anyone, do this. The New York Times.* Retrieved August 8, 2022 from www.nytimes.com/2015/01/11/style/modern-love-to-fall-in-love-with-anyone-do-this.html

The result? The business fails, of course. Because businesses, like relationships, take effort and know-how. The same is true of collaboration.

Here's another parallel: learning matters. I wish every parent took parenting classes. I wish every couple, throuple, and more invested in relationship counseling. I wish every person who ever works with other people—in other words, the overwhelming majority of the workforce—could benefit from professional development aimed at improving their collaborative relationships.

This book offers exactly that.

> *I wish every person who ever works with other people—in other words, the overwhelming majority of the workforce—could benefit from professional development aimed at improving their collaborative relationships.*

The question at hand is how to build healthy and productive collaborative relationships—despite the burn marks left by horrendous experiences in our past, despite that bad taste in our mouths that may suggest it's better to just work alone.

In the chapters that follow, I'll share what I know from the research literature and, more importantly, I will suggest strategies for applying that knowledge to the challenges you face. I'm not here to chastise you or your team for how you've approached your workplace relationships or collaborative work in the past. It's AOK that you and others have a knowledge gap because, well, as I hope was clear from the sections in this chapter, it's not your fault. Also, knowledge gaps are fillable. High five, fellow traveler!

✖ Here's the point

- Collaboration is the process of two or more known individuals working together intentionally to advance a specific shared goal.
- Collaboration is oft sought after because it enables people to accomplish that which would not be possible alone.
- Many people have mixed feelings about collaboration: They know it is ripe with potential *and* they know it can also be a total heartache.
- When we silence the H in collabor(h)ate, we obscure pathways to make working together way more positive for way more people.
- Healthy collaborative relationships are the foundation of effective collaborations.
- Collaboration is difficult both because relationships are difficult and because desperately few people ever receive any substantial training in how to do it well.
- Collaborative relationship skills are learnable.

⑤ Take 5

1. "Collaboration" means different things to different people. What does collaboration mean to you? In what ways does your definition of collaboration differ from mine? Why might a shared definition of collaboration matter to you, your team, and your organization?

2. What three words or phrases best describe your feelings or attitudes toward workplace collaboration? How do your three words and phrases compare to those of others on your team? Why might that variance, or lack thereof, matter?

3. What are the biggest challenges you face when it comes to workplace collaboration?

4. Thinking back over your educational and professional experiences, what sort of training—formal or informal—have you received about how to collaborate well? In what ways has that training informed your collaborative beliefs and behaviors over the years?

5. Within your particular context, what's at stake if your collaborations sizzle versus fizzle for you, your team, your project, and your organization?

Chapter 2
Introducing the Mashek Matrix

Workplace relationships matter

AMERICANS SPEND MORE time working than on all other waking activities *combined*.[20] As the data from Chapter 1 make clear, many of these working hours are spent collaborating with colleagues.

Our collaborative workplace relationships matter, and not just because they help us feel connected and engaged at work. These relationships are also critical vehicles for achieving our most ambitious goals. They're important. We need to invest in them. Yet, rather than putting in the time and effort it takes to build and sustain healthy workplace relationships, people often expect those relationships to somehow develop and grow on their own.

---

[20] U.S. Bureau of Labor Statistics. (n.d.). *Average hours per day spent in selected activities on days worked by employment status and sex, 2021 annual averages*. Retrieved August 8, 2022 from www.bls.gov/charts/american-time-use/activity-by-work.htm

Treating collaborative relationships as an afterthought has consequence. A study conducted by Simpli5 found that 41.2% of respondents felt "friction sometimes while collaborating. Almost a third of respondents had considered leaving their job at some time because of negative team environments, and a sixth of survey respondents were currently considering leaving a job for this reason."[21]

When collaborative work becomes tarnished with tension, eggshells, and trap doors, we carry the stress with us. A 2014 study of nearly 3,000 Norwegian managers found a negative association between the managers' stress levels and the quality of their relationships with their employees: stress levels spike when relationship quality is low. Astrid Richardsen, one of the authors on the paper, notes, "The best thing a manager can do to prevent work stress, is to develop good relationships with the employees at work."[22]

So, how *do* we create and sustain healthy collaborative relationships? Chapter 2 through 5 reveal answers. Before reading further, I encourage you to visit the Digital download section of www.collaborhate.com to complete the Collaborative Relationship Assessment. You will receive two scores, which you can reference as you work through the next few chapters.

Let's start by asking two important questions: How good is your relationship? And, do you and your collaborator influence each other's outcomes? These two questions are at the heart of what it takes to build incredible collaborative relationships. Let's take each in turn.

---

[21] Simpli5. (n.d.). *Organizational dynamics survey: Most businesses have a teamwork problem.* Retrieved August 8, 2022 from www.simpli5.com/resources/organizational-dynamics-survey-teamwork-problem/

[22] BI Norwegian Business School. (2014, August 12). Managers: Less stress when work relationships are good. *ScienceDaily.* Retrieved August 8, 2022 from www.sciencedaily.com/releases/2014/08/140812121737.htm

Relationship quality: How good is your relationship?

Relationship quality lies in the eye of the beholder.

Close relationship scholars define *relationship quality* as "a person's subjective perception that their relationship is relatively good versus bad".[23] In other words, if you think your relationship rocks, then that's that: you're deemed as having high relationship quality.

Seems a bit too simple, right?

But, here's the crazy thing: that subjective assessment of relationship quality predicts all sorts of important real-life things. For example, married individuals who self-report high relationship quality heal more quickly from researcher-inflicted blister wounds (yes, that's a thing) than those who report low relationship quality. They also evidence a lower risk of mortality.

Good relationships are good for us. Intense, right?

Given all the ways relationship quality matters in the lives of individuals, couples, throuples, and so on, perhaps it won't surprise you that relationship quality is the single most studied idea in the close relationships literature.

Through that research, scholars have identified six ingredients, or factors, that make up relationship quality in close romantic relationships. These are: trust, satisfaction, commitment, love,

---

[23] Joel, S., Eastwick, P. W., Allison, C. J., Arriaga, X. B., Baker, Z. G., Bar-Kalifa, E., Bergeron, S., Birnbaum, G. E., Brock, R. L., Brumbaugh, C. C., Carmichael, C. L., Chen, S., Clarke, J., Cobb, R. J., Coolsen, M. K., Davis, J., de Jong, D. C., Debrot, A., DeHaas, E. C., Derrick, J. L., ... Wolf, S. (2020). Machine learning uncovers the most robust self-report predictors of relationship quality across 43 longitudinal couples studies. *Proceedings of the National Academy of Sciences of the United States of America*, 117(32), 19061–19071. https://doi.org/10.1073/pnas.1917036117

intimacy, and passion. While not all those elements are relevant to collaborative relationships, they give a sense of where to start if the goal is to build relationship quality.

So now let's talk about collaborative relationship quality.

In parallel to the established definition of relationship quality, I define *collaborative relationship quality* as your subjective sense of how good or bad your relationship is with a particular collaborator. While collaborative relationship quality is likewise multifaceted, consisting of satisfaction, self-expansion, commitment, trust, and excitement—those facets are empirically less distinct than in the close relationships research, which is why, from here on out, I'll talk about collaborative relationship quality as a single idea.

A simple visual representation of quality appears below, and I'll be building on this simple image in the pages that follow. If you completed the Collaborative Relationship Assessment referenced at the beginning of this chapter, the number labeled "CRQ" is your Collaborative Relationship Quality score. We will talk about how to interpret this value in Chapter 5. For now, know that this number points to your position on the vertical relationship quality dimension, or axis, of something I call the Mashek Matrix.[24] You'll learn more about the Matrix shortly.

Data from the Workplace Collaboration Survey suggests that collaborative relationship quality really matters out there in the real world. Collaborative relationship quality correlates with higher job satisfaction, fewer mental health symptoms, and more favorable attitudes about workplace collaboration.

Collaborative relationship quality continues to predict both job satisfaction and mental health symptoms when controlling for

---

[24] And, yes, I agree this is an oddly self-referential name for something that describes collaborative relationships.

Collaborative relationship quality correlates with higher job satisfaction, fewer mental health symptoms, and more favorable attitudes about workplace collaboration.

overall attitudes toward collaboration. In other words, being in higher quality collaborative relationships is associated with higher job satisfaction and better mental health, *regardless of whether you like collaborating or not.*

Why is this? It could be that high-quality collaborative relationships lead to job satisfaction and mental health. Or, it could be that being in better mental health contributes to being able to create and maintain higher quality collaborative relationships and higher job satisfaction. Or, it could be that other variables, such as a positive workplace culture, lead to both relationship quality and mental health.

Whatever the cause, the pattern is robust: people who have great collaborative relationships are also happier with their jobs, less anxious, and less depressed.

RELATIONSHIP QUALITY AXIS

In addition to varying in quality, relationships also vary in interdependence.

Interdependence: Do you and your collaborator influence each other's outcomes?

I'm going to take a step back to ask a foundational question from my field: What is a relationship?

This is the same definitional question I'd ask students in my *Psychology of Close Relationships* course to mull over on Day 1 to help draw some preliminary boundaries around what would versus would not be covered during the semester.

We'd also explore: What are the defining features of a close relationship? What counts as an intimate relationship? How do you know when you're in a relationship with someone? And my favorite question: Does a relationship continue if one person dies?

We won't dive into all those questions here. I mention them to make the point that this simple four-word question, "What is a relationship?," is surprisingly difficult to answer (and surprisingly fun to discuss over happy hour). But the answer is important. Without it, we can neither systematically study nor improve relationships.

Think about it. You have some sort of relationship with the guy you buy coffee from every morning at the food cart. You have some sort of relationship with your neighbors, friends, and family. You have some sort of relationship with your co-workers. But what features make these "relationships"?

Social psychologist Harold Kelly and his colleagues pondered this question deeply. Here's the answer they came to: two people are in a relationship if they are "interdependent," meaning each person's outcomes are influenced by the other's behavior.[25] How much one person's outcomes are influenced by the other varies, which means interdependence varies.

Here are three questions relationship researchers generally ask to help figure out how interdependent a particular relationship is. As you read these questions, begin thinking about how and when these features are relevant to your workplace relationships, in general, and to your collaborative relationships, in particular.

- **How frequently do the people interact?** The more frequent the interaction, the more interdependent the relationship.
- **Do the individuals influence a diverse range of the other's activities?** The wider array of activities influenced, the more interdependent the relationship.
- **How strong an influence do the individuals have on the other's outcomes?** The stronger the influence, the more interdependent the relationship.

Like any relationship, collaborative relationships vary in their degree of interdependence. As shown below, we can think of interdependence as existing on a continuum from low to high. Interdependence then is the second dimension, or axis, of the Mashek Matrix.

---

[25] Berscheid, E., Snyder, M., & Omoto, A. M. (2004). Measuring closeness: The relationship closeness inventory (RCI) revisited. In D. J. Mashek & A. P. Aron (Eds.), *Handbook of closeness and intimacy* (pp. 81–101). Lawrence Erlbaum Associates Publishers.

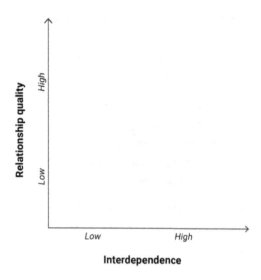

INTERDEPENDENCE AXIS

On the low end, you might see the "divide and conquer" strategy that often typifies "collaboration" on a group assignment in school. Students huddle for 15 minutes after class one day, decide who will prepare which section of the presentation, and then barely talk again until the night before the presentation when everyone dumps their slides together. While the instructor might give a group grade, it counts very little toward the final course grade.

There are, of course, workplace parallels to the "group assignment" model. One person might write the copy for the promotional materials, another person does the layout, and another person decides how to distribute it and to whom. Divide and conquer.

In contrast, other collaborations are intensely interdependent. Not only are you working together non-stop on one or more complicated projects, but your ability to fulfil your responsibilities depends on the work of others. Your risks and rewards are contingent on what other people do, or don't do. You share turf, talent, time, and treasure and are likely optimizing across competing demands and navigating complexity along the way.

This interdependence is both a blessing and a curse. On the plus side, it enables teams to move beyond superficial forms of collaboration to deep collaboration. Such interdependence opens the gate for complex work on ill-defined problems. It enables us to accomplish amazing things.

But, on the other hand, interdependence also means that your work, and the consequences you experience because of that work, becomes profoundly tied to the actions of others on the team. Even if you wanted to, you may not be able to move your own work forward without the other person doing theirs. Or the quality of your contributions may be capped by the timeliness of another's completion. The metrics that feed into your personnel review and thus your earnings may depend, at least in part, on team-based key performance indicators. Your reputation and thus your future opportunities, job prospects, and social network may depend on how the product of this collaboration is received by the client. Your sense of accomplishment, your growth, and your satisfaction with your work may be contingent on the efforts of these collaborators. All told, your collaborators can have a lot of sway in important aspects of your work life. Gulp.

> *This interdependence is both a blessing and a curse. On the plus side, it enables teams to move beyond superficial forms of collaboration to deep collaboration... But, on the other hand, interdependence also means that your work, and the consequences you experience because of that work, becomes profoundly tied to the actions of others on the team.*

Task and outcome interdependence like this means we're not just sharing the rewards of the work, but also the risks. It also means that others have a say in what we do and how we do it, and this can be experienced as a psychologically distressing threat to our autonomy. Interdependence opens up the possibility of getting burned. Big time.

And, yet, if we want to realize the powerful potential afforded by deep collaboration, interdependence is essential.

If you completed the Collaborative Relationship Assessment referenced at the beginning of this chapter, take a look at the number labeled "INT". This is your interdependence score. We will talk about how to interpret this value in Chapter 5. For now, know that this number points to your position on the horizontal interdependence axis of the Mashek Matrix.

To recap: relationships with collaborators vary in both quality and interdependence. The next section gets to the heart of the matter: What happens when we put these two features into conversation?

The Mashek Matrix

These two features of collaborative relating—relationship quality and interdependence—represent the two dimensions of the Mashek Matrix. The *relationship quality* dimension focuses on feelings, the *interdependence* dimension focuses on behaviors. This feelings versus behaviors distinction offers some hints about how we'll adjust those two dimensions, a topic we'll return to in Chapter 3 and Chapter 4.

For this model to be relevant to a particular collaborative relationship, the individuals involved must intend to work together to advance a specific shared goal. They don't need to be doing so well, and they don't have to feel great about it. But, given this is a collaboration model, the assumption heading in is that there's some effort to collaborate underway.

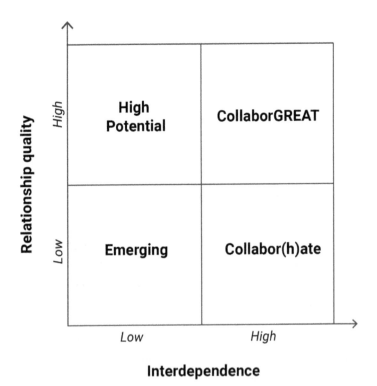

MASHEK MATRIX

As the figure shows, the two dimensions of relationship quality and interdependence each exist on a continuum; for the sake of simplicity we can talk about these features as being "low" or "high," which gives way to four different experiences of collaboration. (If you made a bet with anyone that this business book, like so many other business books, would have a 2 x 2 matrix, please collect your winnings now.)

CollaborGREAT relationships exist when relationship quality and interdependence are both high (top right quadrant). Collaborators are engaged. They're doing A+ work. People know others are counting on them. They take the associated responsibility seriously and behave accordingly. People feel connected to each other and make the effort to see and be responsive to the needs of others. This combination of high relationship quality and high interdependence enables deep collaboration—we truly are able to do together that which none of us could have possibly done alone.

When participants in the Workplace Collaboration Survey were asked to self-select the most influential person within their most important or meaningful collaboration, they selected relationships characterized by both high relationship quality *and* high interdependence. That is, they chose relationships that are truly collaborGREAT.

Now, when relationship quality is high, but interdependence is low, collaborations are *high potential* (top left quadrant). They have in place the critical ingredient of quality, but haven't yet mixed in the powerful amplifier of interdependence to really make the magic happen. People overall enjoy being in the hopper together, but the co-labor, the together work, is likely more superficial than could be possible given the strength of the relationship. You might say these collaborative relationships are underleveraged.

When relationship quality and interdependence are both low (bottom left quadrant), the collaborative relationship is *emerging*. It's unlikely to be particularly fulfilling, nor is it likely to be particularly stressful. It's just kinda there. The work that unfolds in such a relationship is likely superficial and intermittent, meaning individuals in the collaboration can dip in and dash out of the together work. The collaborators may not know, or care about, each other. Collaborators are not likely giving this relationship much consideration beyond the quick touches required through the project.

Finally, in the lower right quadrant we have *collabor(h)ate*. This is the case where relationship quality is in the dumpster, but interdependence is high. This is like having your wagon hitched to somebody else's unpredictable and ill-mannered horse. In this situation, people are at the mercy of teammates whom they don't trust, don't like, and don't want to invest anything extra in. These relationships are incredibly stressful. And we want out.

So, how do you move a relationship from collabor(h)ate to collaborGREAT? We'll dig into that important question in Chapter 5; the pathway may surprise you. But first, we need to talk about the work needed to move along the axes of the Mashek Matrix. How do we improve the quality of our relationships, and thus move up that axis? And, how do we adjust our interdependence and slide along that axis? We will look at these in Chapter 3 and Chapter 4, respectively.

 ## Here's the point

- Collaborative workplace relationships matter both because they help us feel connected and engaged at work and because they are critical vehicles for achieving our most ambitious goals.
- Collaborative relationships vary along two independent dimensions: relationship quality (your subjective sense of how good or bad your relationship is with a particular collaborator) and interdependence (the extent to which each person's outcomes are influenced by the other's behavior).
- The Mashek Matrix puts these two dimensions into conversation with each other, giving rise to four different collaborative experiences: collabor(h)ate, emerging, high potential, and collaborGREAT.

5 Take 5

1. Do you agree or disagree with the claim that we would be wise to invest in the health of our collaborative workplace relationships? Why?

2. "Good relationships are good for you." To what extent do you think this is true within the context of collaborative workplace relationships? Why?

3. Think about a collaborative relationship you are in currently at work. List out all the ways your life is impacted by the other person. As you look over your list, what emotions come up for you? What, if anything, surprises you about the contents of that list or your reactions to it?

4. Think back both to a collaborative relationship from your past that you found particularly fulfilling/positive and to one you found particularly draining/negative. In what ways do those relationships support—versus fail to support—the 2 × 2 matrix presented in this chapter?

5. Like all relationships, collaborative relationships experience ups and downs. If you were to graph the ups and downs of a specific collaborative relationship over time, what shape would that graph show? Steady improvement over time? Volatility? A crashing decline? To what do you attribute changes in the trajectory of your collaborative relationship?

Chapter 3
Understanding relationship quality

K NOWING WHAT RELATIONSHIP quality is and understanding its importance tells us desperately little about how to create and maintain it. Thankfully, substantial existing research points us in the right direction.

This chapter first considers individual difference variables, as these inform experiences in relationships. Then, if you are interested in creating a high-quality collaborative relationship, and if you are able and willing to invest effort into achieving such a relationship, this chapter offers nine strategies to help, each informed by empirical research.

As a heads-up, this chapter is quite long, a testament to the volume of empirically supported options for improving relationship quality. Feel free to bop around from section to section, lingering longer on those sections that resonate most with your needs and situation. The other ideas will be waiting here for you when you're ready. And, thinking ahead to Chapter 5, I encourage you to flag general strategies or specific ideas that appeal to you. We'll make use of those flags in Chapter 5 when we talk about the process for moving from collabor(h)ate to collaborGREAT.

Let's consider: How people differ

Individual differences are characteristics that you as an individual carry with you across situations. The psychological research literature is replete with examples of ways that our individual default settings inform the ways we show up and engage the world, especially our relationships.

Two such individual differences—personality and attachment orientation—are especially relevant to collaborative relationship quality.

The power of personality

Let's start with the personality. When psychologists talk about personality, they mean the characteristic ways individuals tend to think, behave, and feel. These features of the self are relatively stable across our lifespan and across contexts. Personality psychologists talk about five broad features, called the Big Five, which you can remember using the mnemonic OCEAN:

- **O**penness to experience is the tendency to be curious and unconventional;
- **C**onscientiousness is the tendency to be organized and reliable;
- **E**xtraversion is the tendency to be outgoing and energetic;
- **A**greeableness is the tendency to be trusting and appreciative;
- **N**euroticism is the tendency to feel tense and anxious; the opposite of neuroticism is emotional stability, which is how this trait is referred to in the remainder of this section.

I emphasize *tendency* in the bullets above because personality is just that: a predisposition.[26] Personality is not destiny.

Rebekka Weidmann and colleagues reviewed existing research on the connection between personality and romantic relationship quality.[27] They concluded that, of the Big Five personality factors, three seem to be particularly relevant to *romantic* relationship quality: emotional stability, agreeableness, and conscientiousness.

In a nutshell:

- People who are high in *emotional stability* tend to behave, think, and experience emotions in ways that are beneficial to relationships.
- People who are high in *agreeableness* are adept at regulating their emotions and communicating constructively, which is helpful in relationships.
- People who are high in *conscientiousness* tend to manage and control conflict well.

If these patterns hold in collaborative relationships, as well, we'd expect collaborative relationship quality to be predicted by high emotional stability, high agreeableness, and high conscientiousness. It makes intuitive sense that collaborative relationship quality would be advanced when people are relaxed, trusting, appreciative, organized, and reliable.

Matthew Prewett and colleagues conducted a meta-analysis (a study of studies) to explore if the personalities of people on

---

[26] While there are many quizzes out there that claim to assess your personality, few are backed by research. The good news is some are, including the Ten Item Personality Inventory (TIPI), which was designed by Sam Gosling and colleagues. There's a link to the TIPI in the Other Links section of www.collaborhate.com.

[27] Weidmann, R., Ledermann, T., & Grob, A. (2016). The interdependence of personality and satisfaction in couples. *European Psychologist, 21*(4), 284–295. https://doi.org/10.1027/1016-9040/a000261

a team predicted both the behaviors of the team and the team's outcomes.[28] They found that teams' average personality scores on emotional stability, agreeableness, and extraversion correlate with team process, and that this correlation is stronger in situations where the work is especially interdependent (an idea we'll return to in Chapter 4). In other words, when a team is engaged in especially complex work, the team functions better when there's a higher mean level of agreeableness, extraversion, and emotional stability.

So what might this mean for your collaborations?

Let's start with you. As I mentioned before, personality is not destiny, but it is difficult to just will personality to change. So, if you are engaging in habitual modes of thinking, feeling, and behaving that are hurting your collaborative relationships, consider investigating interventions others have found useful. For example, therapy, mindfulness meditation, breathwork, eye movement desensitization and reprocessing, and the adoption of new systems to reinforce positive behaviors may help. These modalities may help short circuit the thoughts, feelings, and behaviors that get in the way of creating high-quality interpersonal connections.

Now, what if you're in a collaboration with someone whose personality is negatively impacting the group and the group's work? This is a difficult situation because, quite frankly, it's impossible to change other people's personalities. But, you can provide feedback to make clear the impact they are having on you, the project, and others. The accountability conversations we discuss later in this chapter can help. And, if you're in a managing or directing role and you see that an employee's emotional volatility, lack of conscientiousness, or lack of agreeableness is impacting the team,

---

[28] Prewett, M. S., Walvoord, A. A. G., Stilson, F. R. B., Rossi, M. E., & Brannick, M. T. (2009). The team personality-team performance relationship revisited: The impact of criterion choice, pattern of workflow, and method of aggregation. *Human Performance, 22*(4), 273–296. https://doi.org/10.1080/08959280903120253

you must do something about it. Have the tough conversation, offer resources, set up the performance improvement plan, and, if needed, transition them from the team. Side-stepping tough conversations or avoiding making tough decisions allows that person to continue wreaking havoc on other individuals and on team dynamics, which hurts everyone's ability to do their work, as well as your company's culture and bottom line.

In addition, monitor your reactions to others. If you find yourself getting tense when a colleague lists off the myriad ways the project could go wrong, take a deep breath, and remind yourself that they're not doing this to get under your skin or to be a wet blanket. They do this because they are wired to see risk differently than you. It can be helpful to remind yourself of the value this person brings to the team vis à vis "looking around corners" to anticipate the unexpected.

It's also fairly clear that agreeableness is a valuable resource in all sorts of relationships. If you happen to have an agreeable personality, know that this is an asset you bring into your collaborations. Though, keep in mind that agreeableness needn't mean one agrees with everything all the time. Indeed, too much "going with the flow" can undermine a team's work; constructive tension is important to optimize decisions.

Attachment anxiety and avoidance

Attachment orientation is a second individual difference that's very relevant to workplace relationships.

Because of our relationship experiences in childhood, we develop beliefs about how relationships work, including whether other people can be counted on to provide support and whether we're comfortable depending on them to do so.

For example, imagine a child whose caregiver is able and willing to respond to the child's distress in predictable, reliable ways over time and across situations. When the kiddo shares that she is hungry, the caregiver provides nourishment. If she falls on the playground, the caregiver soothes the scraped knee and the shaken confidence, then encourages the kiddo to get back out there and give it another go. That child learns both that others can be counted on for support and that she is worthy of that support.

In contrast, imagine a child whose caregiver is largely absent or perhaps physically present but so distracted by their own challenges that they don't notice, or are incapable of responding to, the child's hunger or injury. Over time, that child comes to believe that others cannot be counted on for help or that she is inherently unworthy of care; the child may come to believe that it's better to go it alone. Or, if the quality and availability of support are intermittent and impossible to predict, the kiddo may become hyper attuned to any indicators that signal the likelihood of the caregiver's responsiveness.

These expectations and beliefs, or working models, are with us, as psychiatrist John Bowlby so powerfully put it, "from the cradle to the grave."[29] They're like a pair of goggles bolted over our eyes. We can't take them off even if we wanted to, which means they are with us in adulthood, too.

These working models color our experiences of our workplace relationships. What you notice, what you care about, what you worry about, the stories you tell about yourself and others, how you react in good times and bad—all are tied to this important individual difference.

There are two dimensions in adult attachment: anxiety and avoidance.

People who are high in attachment *anxiety* feel uncertain about the availability and responsiveness of others. Evidence suggests

[29] Bowlby J. (1969/1982) *Attachment and loss: Vol 1 attachment.* Basic Books.

these individuals are especially likely to seek feedback about their performance in workplace groups.[30] People who are high in attachment *avoidance* are uncomfortable depending on others. That, of course, makes it difficult for them to truly trust that their collaborators will do what they say they're going to do.[31]

Like personality, our attachment orientations are rather stable over time. This means there's no simple way to change your attachment orientation just by willing it to be so. If you find yourself worrying that others won't support you or that others simply can't be counted on, introspect about your beliefs and expectations regarding others' responsiveness and your comfort leaning on others. Resist the urge to micromanage others' work, giving them a chance to prove you wrong about their dependability. A skilled therapist can support this exploration and can help you think about how those beliefs, again many of which stem from your earliest relationship experiences, might no longer be serving your interests at work or elsewhere.

Individuals who are low on both attachment anxiety and avoidance believe they are inherently worthy of others' care and concern and are comfortable leaning on others. If you could use a gentle nudge to help yourself think more securely, clinical psychologist Jessica Borelli and her colleagues developed a powerful relational savoring intervention.[32] While originally developed for use in therapeutic and research settings, this intervention can also serve as

[30] Yip, J., Ehrhardt, K., Black, H., & Walker, D. O. (2018). Attachment theory at work: A review and directions for future research. *Journal of Organizational Behavior*, *39*(2), 185–198. https://doi.org/10.1002/job.2204
[31] If you're curious where you fall on the anxiety and avoidance dimensions, check out the Experiences in Close Relationships scale by Kelly Brennan and colleagues. There's a self-scoring version linked in the Other Links section of www.collaborhate.com.
[32] Borelli, J. L., Smiley, P. A., Kerr, M. L., Hong, K., Hecht, H. K., Blackard, M. B., Falasiri, E., Cervantes, B. R., & Bond, D. K. (2020). Relational savoring: An attachment-based approach to promoting interpersonal flourishing. *Psychotherapy*, *57*(3), 340–351. https://doi.org/10.1037/pst0000284

Six steps for relational savoring

Step 1. Think about a time when a collaborator responded sensitively to your needs (or when you responded sensitively to their needs) or when a collaborator empowered you to take on a risk or challenge (or when you encouraged them to do the same).

Step 2. Describe the memory in as much detail as possible. As Borelli and colleagues explain, "describe what time of day the event occurred, what the other person was wearing, what the air was like, and what they could hear, smell, taste, see, and touch…bring the scene to mind as vividly as possible."

Step 3. Describe the emotions and bodily sensations you either associate with the memory or re-experience as you recall the details around that memory.

Step 4. Explore what meaning or insights bubble up for you as you engage in the savoring. For example, you might ask yourself, "What's important here that I want to hold on to?" or "What does this memory suggest about me or the people in my world?"

Step 5. Explore the connection between that past memory and your future collaborative relationships. For example, "How might this connection affect your relationship with your collaborator in the future"? or "How do you think this relationship might empower you in the future?"

Step 6. Let your thoughts wander freely for a few minutes and jot down anything else that comes to mind about the memory or the feelings it brings up for you. Borelli and colleagues say this open-ended time promotes deeper processing.

fodder for self-reflection and journaling to help people, regardless of their attachment orientation, feel more secure in their relationships and to reap the benefits of that felt security. The Toolbox above overviews these six steps of relational savoring, framed for a collaborative relationship at work.

Nine strategies to increase relationship quality

So how do you create high-quality relationships? Here are nine empirically-supported strategies for increasing relationship quality.

Set clear expectations

Expectations play a hugely important role in any relationship because, when unmet, they set the stage for disappointment, hurt feelings, and—yes—low relationship quality. Your collaborators are not mind readers. And, guess what, neither are you. So here's the solution: You talk about it.

If you want to reduce the likelihood of dashed hopes in your workplace collaborations, set aside time at the beginning of a collaboration to make expectations explicit and to co-create an understanding of the norms that will govern the shared work. Then, revisit these agreements if and when they aren't met or as part of a regularly scheduled relationship maintenance check-up. (Seriously, it's OK to put such things on the calendar.)

Having expectation-setting conversations is non-negotiable and everyone in the collaboration co-owns responsibility for making it happen. If your team hasn't had this conversation, it's perfectly appropriate—and highly advised—to say something like, "I know we all want to knock this project out of the park and to be a great team along the way. Let's discuss how we're going to work together."

Expectation-setting conversations generally take one of three forms, which vary in depth and complexity: a conversation to form basic agreements, a structured series of questions, and an in-depth assessment.

First, you could have a general conversation around the question "What agreements shall we make about how we're going to work together?" General principles of interaction will emerge here such as "do what we say we're going to do," "do A+ level work on anything that will be seen by someone external to the team," "be punctual," and "ask for help when you need it."

Second, you could use the questions in the box below to help make explicit some of the most foundational practices of working together. These questions work well across a range of situations. For example, I'd encourage my college students to work through them when launching group projects and I personally use them in kick-off calls with clients.

 10 questions to quickly set expectations

Question 1. What channel should we use for team communication? Email, text, Slack? Pick a channel and stick with it so everyone will know where to look for updates, past conversations, drafts, resources, and so on.

Question 2. What's your contact information? Once your group has selected a communication platform, get everyone's contact information. Send a test message to make sure everyone can indeed reach each other. It's worth verifying contact info before someone is inadvertently cut out of the communication loop.

Question 3. What's our expected response time? Do we all agree to reply to questions posed to the group within two hours? Two days? Set a standard that will work with everyone's existing commitments and with cultural norms within your organization, if relevant. Don't leave your team hanging: Honor what the group decides.

Question 4. Where shall we store shared documents? Google Drive, DropBox, the file drawer in Bob's office? Pick a spot everyone has access to. Set up a basic folder structure. Use it. On the off chance a team member falls ill or has to disappear for a family emergency, everyone will have access to the information and work they need to keep the project moving forward.

Question 5. When shall we hold our standing meetings and where shall we meet? Pick a standing meeting time that will work with everyone's existing commitments. Will you meet daily? Weekly? Set the time. Hold it as sacred. Pick a single location (e.g., Maria's Zoom room; Google Meet; the coffee shop). No need to waste precious minutes re-negotiating meeting times or wandering around your co-working space looking for your team. Create a calendar invite with the location. Add everyone to the invite. Be there.

Question 6. What type of work do you enjoy most? Group members each bring real talent to the shared task. Knowing what type of work individuals are drawn to can help the group identify the team's strengths and needs, as well as determine roles and responsibilities. Some people love conducting research. Others love writing. Keep in mind that, while everyone will ideally have opportunities to contribute their strengths, they may also be interested in developing new skills.

Question 7. What do you want to get out of this experience? While group work sometimes feels like a huge undertaking, it can serve group members' broader professional development goals. Take a minute to explore what those might be so you can design the work in a way that supports the individuals who make up the group. What skills do you most want to learn or practice, for example?

Question 8. What level of polish would you like to work toward? Is this a "get it done" or a "make it perfect" situation? It's good to know upfront if you have some group members who are just looking to pass an assignment versus others who want to ace it, for example. Knowing this in advance will help your group decide how to allocate work and can help prevent frustration. Similarly, a management consultant in the UK asks, "Is this a 'Rolls Royce or a Mini?'" to help teams understand the level of effort and other resources to be invested in the project.

Question 9. Who needs to do what by when? Maintain a single list of action items that's accessible to everyone in the group. This might live within a subscription to a project management tool or on a wall populated with brightly colored sticky notes. During meetings, keep track of who has stepped up for certain tasks and record by when they said that task will be completed. At the top of each and every meeting, review the action items that were due to ensure they have been done. Accountability is key to a positive experience.

Question 10. What else should we know about you? Take some time to get to know the individuals who make up your group. What else are they juggling? How do they like to spend their nonwork time? What are they passionate about? Knowing group members as people helps establish trust and rapport, and those are critical ingredients to positive and productive collaboration.

The general approaches above work well in a lot of cases, but sometimes more specificity is desired. That is where the third option comes in.

There are hundreds of possible topics you could set expectations around. For example, here's a partial list of issues you could potentially discuss regarding the single topic of meetings: the purpose of the meeting, who should attend and why, who will agendize meetings, who can contribute agenda items, how and when the call for agenda items will occur, who will create meeting artifacts (e.g., notes), where those artifacts will be stored, what level of preparation is expected for meetings, whether prework is expected, how far in advance prework will be distributed, level of engagement expected at meetings, where meetings will be held, video meeting protocols (e.g., cameras on, OK to have email or other notifications open, OK to have back channel chats going on), how meeting time will be structured, who decides if a meeting will be canceled, and how far in advance such calls will be made.

A similarly lengthy list could be generated for important topics like project management, decision making, conflict, communications, and so on.

I highly doubt you have the time or interest in having a deep conversation about *all* these topics for each of your collaborations. Heck, some of them are likely not even relevant to you. But some of them will be relevant, and some of them may even be critically important to your team's success.

Identify which topics are important enough to your team to warrant specific expectations; you would ideally do this in conversation with others on the team, but it is possible for one person (for example, the team lead) to make the first pass here.

Once you know which topics warrant expectations, go through the list again and indicate whether expectations for that item are "entirely absent," "present, though unstated, implicit, or assumed," "stated explicitly, though generally vague or fuzzy," or "stated explicitly and are generally clear and specific."

Once you have your list of important topics around which there needs to be expectations, and you've discerned which topics already have clear and specific expectations, turn your attention to clarifying expectations around the remaining important topics.

Here's the framing question to discuss with your collaborators: "What expectations do we have about (insert topic)?" Talk through the specifics to level set.

Document these expectations in writing. Share the document with the team. If a new person joins the team, make sure they get a copy of the document and invite a conversation about its contents.

You might be thinking, "Holy smokes, this sounds painfully tedious." Yes, it's a ton of work. And it takes time to do well. My three pieces of advice are:

- Cluster the topics into categories to see if it makes sense to set expectations for a smaller number of clusters rather than for each topic individually.
- Have in place a decision about how decisions will be made so that the group doesn't spend time down unnecessary rabbit holes.
- Think about the cost of inaction (if you don't have these conversations now, how might it cost you down the road?).

While it doesn't matter much which approach you take to co-creating expectations, it is important that expectations are discussed. If you don't have these conversations early on, you're introducing future risk in terms of team dynamics, project quality, reputation, bottom line, and beyond.

Organizational psychologist Liane Davey brilliantly hits home why expectation-setting conversations are critical. She refers to it as "The Valentine's Day Effect."[33]

A friend came to Liane with an elaborate vision for how their partner could show their love on Valentine's Day. When Liane asked, "Have you told them?," the response was always, "No, if they really loved me, they'd know." As Liane said, "Yeah, so that doesn't work. All I could say was, 'Why are you setting up the person you love to disappoint you?'"

The same goes for your collaborators: Why set them up to disappoint you? Take the imaginary skill of mind-reading off the table; have the expectation-setting conversations. And, take personal responsibility for contributing to those conversations by sharing your preferences and needs.

Behave accordingly

Of course, it's not enough to have clear expectations. You also have to behave accordingly. Failure to do so tanks relationship quality.

For example, it's not enough just to know you're supposed to show up prepared for meetings. You actually have to show up prepared for meetings. It's not enough just to say you hold another person's anxieties in confidence. You actually have to do so. Fulfilling expectations drives relationship quality.

Take another look at the topics for which your team has set expectations. Ask yourself to what extent are your behaviors consistent with your team's expectations on each of these? In the expectation-setting workshops I do with teams, I ask people to answer this question using the response options Never, Rarely, Sometimes, Usually, and Always.

---

[33] Davey, L. (2019, February 17). *What teams can learn from Valentine's Day*. Liane Davey. Retrieved August 8, 2022 from www.lianedavey.com/what-teams-can-learn-from-valentines-day/

Now, if you really want to know if you're fulfilling expectations, ask others on your team to rate you in the same way. A facilitated 360 collaboration assessment can help garner anonymous, actionable insights. While it may be difficult to put yourself out there for review, there really is no better way to figure out how you're doing on the behavioral expectation front.

If you or others perceive you as falling short on any of the behaviors, ask why that might be. Be honest with yourself here. Is it because you object to the expectations and thus have no intention of upholding them? Is it a motivational issue? Or, perhaps you don't understand why this particular behavior is valued by the team. Or, maybe you don't have access to the skills or resources to do that particular thing. Or, perhaps your understanding of what it means to "come prepared" differs from how others understand it. It's also possible that, while you are in fact doing the expected things, others are unable to see your work because it occurs outside their awareness.

The answers you come to will point you in the right direction in terms of next steps. You may need to ask the team for help clarifying an expectation. Or, you may need to ask your supervisor to help you brainstorm ways to onboard the needed resources or to rearrange your commitments to provide the capacity necessary to do the work at the level expected. Maybe you simply need to be more deliberate in making your work visible.

Importantly, your good behaviors will increase the likelihood of others' good behaviors. You'll create a virtuous cycle on the team by taking the team's expectations seriously. So my advice here: act first. If you're not behaving well, then work on changing your behaviors before asking others to do the same.

Avoid telling yourself stories

Our brains are storytelling machines. They are wired to make sense of the world's messiness, making all the happenstance a bit less overwhelming and a bit more navigable by creating the impression that life is predictable.

When it comes to collaboration, this storytelling can be a big problem.

When someone doesn't behave as expected, or when something goes wrong, our brains immediately start asking "Why?" Our brains are quite adept at coming up with rich stories based on thin evidence.

Misunderstandings, negative feelings, and counterproductive interactions kick up when we jump into negative storytelling about our collaborators:

- They didn't show up on time for the meeting because they're inconsiderate jerks.
- The process they proposed makes zero sense because they're so freakin' clueless about how the business really works.
- The draft report they wrote for the client was of embarrassingly low quality because they don't give a damn about this project or their impact on your reputation.
- They didn't reply to the text message because they're ignoring you.

Gulp. What if:

- They were late because of horrendous traffic on the freeway.
- Their process didn't make sense because you had neglected to communicate key information about the context and constraints.

- They understood that the draft was just for the two of you to see and wanted to get as much clay on the proverbial table before sculpting the product.
- They did reply to the text, but it evaporated en route to your phone.[34]

While storytelling is normal, jumping to conclusions can undermine healthy relationships, a point well made by a director in social services. She shared a dramatic story of a colleague who blew up an important interdepartmental collaboration that would have landed a huge grant to make services available to more people in need. The reason the colleague blew up the collaboration: she had conjured ornate and very negative stories about the source of the money, why the partner department had interest in it, and the impact that money would have on her department. "Because of her, because of her off-the-rails, out-of-proportion reaction, the whole thing blew up."

The time to intervene in storytelling is way before a big blow up. One start-up founder encourages everyone on his team to ask, "Am I giving the other person the benefit of the doubt?" He said, "I found myself asking that question over and over again in relationships when something felt off. And the answer was always 'no.'"

When you notice you've got a tidy answer at the ready about why a collaborator behaved a certain way or why something negative happened, take a breath. Then slow down the storytelling by asking yourself questions such as those in the box below.

---

[34] I have lost count of the number of times this has happened to messages I send. If you don't hear back, reach out through another channel.

Questions to ask yourself to slow down storytelling

- What here is fact, fiction, fictionalized fact (i.e., a truth that I'm stretching or overstating), and factualized fiction (i.e., conjecture that I'm stating as if true)?
- What situational factors might be at play?
- In what ways might my information about the situation be incomplete or inaccurate?
- What assumptions am I making about others, their abilities, intentions, values, and beliefs?
- Can I come up with at least five other possible explanations for this situation?

What purpose do these questions serve? First, merely asking yourself these questions serves as a reminder that we can rarely know why something happened just by glancing at the situation. Second, these questions invite us to view the situation through different lenses, which equips us to see additional texture and nuance. Third, doing the "thinking work" involved in exploring these questions holds at bay the hot emotions that can easily kick up when we think we've been wronged.

When emotions are hot, it's hard to think or behave constructively. Many of the strategies described in this chapter and the next will feel next to impossible once your blood starts boiling. We need to either prevent the hot emotions from flooding us in the first place or summon the wherewithal to remove ourselves from the situation so we can calm down before re-entering the conversation.

The book *Crucial conversations* offers wonderful advice on how to do both.[35]

Left unchecked in our heads and hearts, the negative stories we tell ourselves about others impact relationship quality in at least four ways:

- It's hard to feel great about a relationship when you think the other person is a clueless inconsiderate jerk.
- You're more likely to interpret the person's future behavior negatively (think the opposite of rose-colored glasses).
- The narrative in your mind makes it more difficult for you to even notice, much less integrate, contrary evidence (confirmation bias strikes again!).
- Those stories drive the emotions you feel.

This last point warrants repeating: the stories we tell ourselves give rise to the emotions we feel. If you've been in therapy or have worked with mindfulness teachers, you've probably heard some version of the saying, "emotions are not reality." They might say, "feelings aren't facts" or "your feelings are real, but they aren't reality." At the heart of these sayings is the insight that our emotions are the result of the stories we tell ourselves. And, unfortunately, it's easy to misconstrue the emotions we feel as evidence that the stories we have told ourselves are accurate.

Stories and emotions, then, create a vicious cycle that can make it difficult to engage constructively when a collaborator violates expectations.

> The stories we tell ourselves give rise to the emotions we feel... And, unfortunately, it's easy to misconstrue the emotions we feel as evidence that the stories we have told ourselves are accurate.

[35] Grenny, J., Patterson, K., McMillan, R., Switzler, A., & Gregory, E. (2021). *Crucial conversations: Tools for talking when stakes are high* (3rd ed). McGraw Hill.

Embrace accountability

There will be times when you and your collaborators will violate the shared expectations. The question is how to respond in those situations to hold yourself and others accountable, while also protecting the fabric of the relationship.

Let's start with the situation where you realize you're not going to be able to fulfill an expectation. Perhaps you looked at your work for the week and cannot see a way to hit the submission deadline you had promised your co-authors. What do you do?

- **Communicate the snag as early as possible.** Generally, the negative impacts of a dropped ball rise exponentially as deadlines draw near. I once had a co-author who kept assuring me he was drafting a key section of our paper, but kept putting off my requests to see a draft. Finally, the night before the submission was due, he called to say he hadn't been able to complete the task. That late-in-the-game disclosure, of course, made it next to impossible for me to pivot my pieces or to step in to support his struggle with any grace. The editor was not pleased with the impact our now-late delivery had on the copy editors, the designers, and the marketing team.

- **Be direct.** Rather than cloaking your "I screwed up" disclosure in vacuous jargon, say what you really mean. "I will be unable to meet the January 31 deadline" is a lot better than "Due to an unfortunate constellation of unavoidable circumstances across the organization, it looks like there might be a slight hiccup in the timeline that we had sketched out." Huh? A collaborator once called me to talk about a new future opportunity to work together, which—come to find out after a series of rather awkward interactions—was his attempt to let me know he needed to terminate our existing work together. As my mind-reading powers were turned off that day, I had no idea what he was trying to say.

- **Apologize and make clear you understand the impact.** Saying you're sorry is important, but it's not enough. You also want to demonstrate that you understand what you're sorry for—you're sorry for negatively impacting the project and other people. Be specific here. "I'm sorry I won't be able to meet the January 31 deadline. I realize my planning error impacts your schedule and that you had moved your work around last week to prioritize this project. I also realize my lateness means our submission will not qualify for the juried competition, which means our company can't possibly win the industry prize."

- **Offer solutions.** Don't stop at the apology: offer strategies to bridge the gap. Make clear what you are able and willing to do to make amends. For example, "Looking ahead to later this month, I see another project that could be moved into Q2, where I have more capacity. That means I can finish our paper then. And, so that you don't also have to move around your schedule, I would like to take on the final read through and editing so you don't have to."

- **Ask for help.** Invite the other person to help create a solution. "What do you think about this proposed solution? What other ideas do you have for mitigating the impact of my error?"

- **Reaffirm that you value the other person and your relationship with them.** "I value you, your work, and our relationship. I know my behaviors have had an impact on all three. I am sorry."

Now, what about the situation where a collaborator violates an expectation? How do you hold them accountable?

- **Succinctly describe the difference between what you expected and what you saw.** For example, if a collaborator arrives late to a meeting and seems disengaged, you might say: "Deb, at the beginning of the project, the team talked about our shared expectations around meetings, including punctual attendance and full engagement. You arrived ten minutes late to today's meeting and were looking at your phone instead of watching Alex's presentation."

- **Own your reaction.** As we talked about in the previous section, it's easy to slide into explanations about why your colleague was late and disengaged. If you notice any stories kicking up for you, share them, but do so in a tentative manner. "When I saw this, a worry bubbled up for me that maybe you're second guessing your commitment to the project."

- **Name the impact.** When a collaborator's behavior affects others or the project in some way, it's important to make those impacts visible. "Alex shared great insights that will be relevant to your piece of the project and now you're missing those, which means the project may end up less coherent than what's possible."

- **Invite the other person to contribute their insights.** Ask your colleague to share how they see the situation. You might say, "What was going on for you today?" or "How do you see it?"

- **Invite solutions.** You can then ask, "What ideas do you have for remedying the situation?" Or, "What changes can you commit to going forward?"

Now, if a collaborator has pointed out that you have violated an expectation, thank them for holding you accountable. And, offer your solution: "I'm going to go watch the recording of the presentation now, then apologize to Alex directly as well as let them know that I have watched the presentation and how I see those ideas feeding into my piece of the project."

Your receptivity to feedback is critical to the health of your collaborative relationship. If you react defensively or if you off-load the blame for poor performance or dropped balls on others, you miss out on the opportunity to become better at your work, undermine the quality of the shared work, and erode the fabric of trust in the relationship.

Many of the people I interviewed talked about the importance of receiving feedback well. One CEO talked about a team member who interpreted all feedback as him creating a hostile work environment and the heavy lift such accusations caused for the organization. He said, "Calling you out for not doing what you promised to do and have been asked to do five times since is not me creating a hostile work environment, it's me holding you accountable."

In each of the situations above—when you realize you've made a flub, when you observe a collaborator making a flub, and when you're called on your flub—it's critical to hold in mind the ultimate goal. Imagine a hiker who veers off trail. Assuming they truly want to make it to a particular destination, veering off trail works against their ability to meet their goal. The same is true with accountability. When we hold ourselves and others accountable to shared expectations, we're increasing the likelihood we will be able to get to our destination.

And, finally, forgive and move on. We all make mistakes. And it sometimes takes a lot of courage to admit those mistakes and to make amends. Rather than carrying the weight of a grudge on your shoulders, give forgiveness and move on. Or, in the case of large or oft-repeated transgressions, take the necessary action via the appropriate channels, but still forgive and move on.

Be responsive

Everyone has needs, goals, values, preferences, wants, abilities, interests, worries, dreams, and so on. While some of these core features of the self may be more salient than others in the workplace, they are with us wherever we go.

In high-quality relationships, we both respond to the other person's needs and notice when they are responsive to ours. We both see the other person for who they are and feel seen by them. This responsiveness is a key driver of relationship quality.

John Gottman, a giant in the field of marital therapy, notes that "Couples often ignore each other's emotional needs out of mindlessness, not malice."[36] The same is true in workplace collaborations. We often get so busy with our own stuff that we neglect to pay attention to the needs of those with whom we work. Our collaborative relationships suffer as a consequence.

Try to notice and respond to your collaborator's needs. Over time, the other person will come to see that you have their back and, assuming they are likewise making the effort to be responsive to your needs, you will come to see that they have yours. This mutual responsiveness builds trust and connection, which will steady the relationship when it encounters challenges (and it will surely encounter challenges because, well, fallible humans are involved).

> *We often get so busy with our own stuff that we neglect to pay attention to the needs of those with whom we work. Our collaborative relationships suffer as a consequence.*

So how can you put this principle into practice?

First, simply be aware that how you act in small, daily interactions matters. Casual chats by the coffee machine, the settling-in minutes before the meeting, and even the sign-off you use in an email are all opportunities to demonstrate micro-moments of responsiveness. They matter.

---

[36] Gottman, J. M., & Silver N. (1999). *The seven principles for making marriage work: A practical guide from the country's foremost relationship expert.* Random House/Crown/Harmony.

Second, make an effort to truly see your collaborator. What do their actions and words say about their needs, goals, values, preferences, wants, abilities, interests, worries, dreams, and so on? These core features may be communicated in incredibly small ways. Pay attention.

For example, you may notice your collaborator consistently uses a very specific convention to name the files in your shared drive. Might this communicate a value around organization or a concern about losing important information? While on a video call with them you notice a pile of kids' sporting gear on the floor. What might this communicate about the commitments they're juggling?

Other times, these core features may be communicated more overtly. For example, your collaborator might share that they had a negative personnel review last quarter and that they're feeling especially vulnerable around task completion. What might this disclosure tell you about how best to highlight this collaborator's contributions in an upcoming team meeting? What else might be at stake for your collaborator in this project (e.g., job security, financial security)?

Third, demonstrate responsiveness to your collaborator through both your words and actions, both publicly and privately.

In the case of the collaborator who names files in a specific way, you can demonstrate responsiveness by saying something like, "Would you mind walking me through your file-naming convention so I can use it, too, to help us stay organized?"

You can demonstrate that you "see" the soccer parent by saying, "It looks like your kiddo is into soccer? That's so fun! I love that my guy is into baseball, but it sure is a juggle to get him to all the practices and games." (This response subtly communicates, "I get it" while also revealing something about you, a relationship-building move we'll return to in the next section.)

If a project timeline starts to slide due to a client's lack of engagement, you might be able to demonstrate responsiveness to your collaborator by, when the slipped timeline comes up at a team meeting, casually saying something like, "Roberto and I are rocking our work on this; we are eager to hear back from the client so we can take this project over the line."

Finally, watch closely for what Gottman calls bids for responsiveness. Collaborators will sometimes make subtle bids for responsiveness, essentially signaling, "Hey, I could use a bit of support right now." Be alert for those bids and use them as an opportunity to provide responsiveness and build relationship quality.

A collaborator who says, "I don't see how this new request can possibly fit in" may be communicating stress about the feasibility of the work. You might reply, "Let's make time for huddle this afternoon to sort it out."

A collaborator who logs out of a meeting quickly after getting an earful from the boss might text you with a vague note like, "That was interesting." Checking in with a simple, "How are you holding up?" communicates that you understand that call might have been a tough one.

Perhaps surprisingly, being responsive to positive disclosures, a process known as capitalization, contributes to relationship quality, too. When a collaborator shares good news with you, express your interest and enthusiasm. "That is fabulous news! Congratulations. I'd love to hear what you're thinking for next steps, if you have time?"

In relationships characterized by high responsiveness, individuals can see and monitor the other's needs and interests; they understand the nature of those needs and why they're important to the other person, and they behave in a way that supports the realization of those needs.

Bring the donuts

Whether you're initiating relationships with new colleagues or looking to strengthen existing connections, communal norms offer a pathway for creating satisfying connections in the workplace and beyond. What's a communal norm, you ask? I'll get to that in a moment, but first, let's do a little thought experiment.

Imagine a marriage in which the individuals track each other's respective contributions to the household. "I put gas in the car last time, so it's your turn to do it this time." "You cleared the dinner table three nights in a row, so I am in debt and must catch up." "I spent $150 on groceries this week and you only spent $125 last week; you owe me $12.50." Cue Venmo.

If this relationship sounds more transactional than close, there's good reason: Tit-for-tat tracking of contributions and benefits is a hallmark of what social scientists call an exchange relationship. In such relationships, members give benefits with the expectation that a comparable benefit will be provided in quick return.

Exchange relationships exist throughout our daily lives. We pay the bus driver in exchange for a ride across town. We pay our gym membership in exchange for use of the facility. Employers pay our salary in exchange for our thinking and doing. Indeed, exchange relationships are normal, appropriate, and welcomed in a lot of situations.

But, get this: We notice, and dislike, when someone treats us with exchange norms when we either think our relationship is on friendlier terms or when we want it to be so.

For example, I once thought I had become decent work friends with a colleague. One day we decided to bop over to the coffee shop on a break. Once there, she realized she had left her wallet in the office. No worries. I picked up the tab. Not a big deal, right? Well, upon our return to the office, she dug out her wallet, raced to the ATM, got cash, and promptly payed me back. (Yes, this was prior to Venmo's arrival to the scene.) Guess what? She just told me that she sees our relationship as governed by tit-for-tat sensibilities. That stung. Why?

Well, exchange norms aren't the only game in town.

Other relationships are governed by what social scientists call communal norms. In these relationships, we give benefits to others to support their welfare, not to gain offsetting benefits for ourselves. Simple examples of this include texting your spouse when you make an impromptu stop at the market to ask if they need anything, helping a neighbor dig their car out after a snowstorm, or bringing a dozen donuts (or a healthier alternative) into the office as a "just because" treat for your co-workers.

In communal relationships, we pitch in, not because we must or because we owe someone a favor, but because we see an opportunity to contribute positively to someone else's world.

And we understand that others who treat us with communal sensibilities value us and want to be in a relationship with us. This is why it stings when a co-worker trips over themselves to repay you a small favor when you thought you were in Communalandia: They're telling you that, no, in fact, you are squarely in the exchange neighborhood.

So, how exactly might one go about applying this principle in the workplace to improve relationship quality? Quite simply, look for small ways to bring a bit of light to others' worlds and do so with no expectation of repayment. While this tendency comes naturally to givers,[37] anyone can enact communal norms with a bit of intentionality.

---

[37] Grant, A. (2013). *Give and take: Why helping others drives our success.* Penguin Books.

Take the initiative to generate the calendar invite. Do the time zone math when sharing your availability so your colleague doesn't need to do the translation. Volunteer to open your calendar a bit more to avoid meeting while your colleague will be with their kids. Volunteer to take meeting notes for the crew. Offer to write the first draft of the document. Share the article you think others might find value in. And, yes: bring the donuts.

All of these are small ways to manifest the communal spirit within the operational constraints of the workplace. I would advise against trying all of these right out of the gate. Just pick one or two that you feel comfortable doing within your workplace. See how it feels. Notice how others respond.

Now, one of the hallmarks of communal relationships is that we don't track the respective inputs and outputs of each person. But, of course, you don't want to become the doormat who does everything for everyone else and who never benefits from reciprocal acts.

It's worth noting here a distinction between communal norms versus communal relationships. The examples above are ideas for engaging communal norms with an eye toward creating more communal relationships. If the relationships are not already communal-leaning, it makes sense to pay a bit of attention to how others respond to the communal gestures. Ideally, your efforts fuel a virtuous cycle in the office, spurring others to contribute to the shared pool of communal care over time. But, if you've been at this for a while and, come to find out, you're the only one contributing benefits to the common good, it may be time to reassess. You can gracefully point out imbalances (e.g., "I took notes last meeting, so let's have someone else step up this time"), pull back on your efforts, or highlight the small actions you see and appreciate from others (e.g., "OK, who added all those citations to the report?! Thank you!").

Be on the lookout, too, for gendered dynamics that pigeonhole communal behavior as being "women's work" (e.g., acts that have an administrative or care-taking bent, like taking notes or providing food) or "men's work" (e.g., acts that have a physical or mechanical bent, like changing the water in the bubbler or fixing the printer). Weaving the communal fabric is a responsibility we can all share, regardless of confining gender socialization.

Talk about yourself

Self-disclosure creates closeness; closeness, in turn, is associated with trust and prosocial action. If you'd like to nudge collaborative relationship quality, share a bit of yourself with your colleagues. Take the risk of being seen and of seeing others.

It's important that disclosures be appropriate for the setting. Talking at work about your kids' cute antics? Yes. Talking about your colonoscopy prep? No.

Also, monitor for reciprocal disclosure. In a classic study designed to experimentally generate interpersonal closeness, researchers guided pairs of strangers through a series of reciprocal self-disclosure conversations.[38] This short, one-hour task resulted in participants feeling closer to their interaction partner—a total stranger—than the typical closest relationship of 30% of similar people.

If you share something about yourself, make space for others to do the same in their own way and in their own time. If others don't readily share, don't push. Their reticence might be a sign that they're not quite ready for, or perhaps not interested in, a deeper relationship. And, if someone shares something with you, reciprocate in kind, if you feel comfortable doing so.

Be mindful of what you're disclosing. The interpersonal process model of intimacy suggests that, while factual disclosures can

---

[38] (Aron et al., 1997)

help create closeness ("My computer crashed this morning..."), emotional disclosures do so more powerfully ("... and I am devastated knowing I lost all the work I had done on an important paper").[39]

And, while you might be tempted to really open up and share something deeply personal, remember that it takes time to build the intimacy required for such disclosures to land safely. You know how SCUBA divers can get the bends if they ascend too quickly from a dive? Same thing goes for self-disclosure: too much too fast can leave others feeling yucky. Go slowly. Nobody wants a case of the disclosure bends.

The experimental study mentioned above was intentionally structured to begin with mundane disclosures (e.g., "What would constitute a perfect day for you?"). The questions then transition into slightly more self-revealing disclosures (e.g., "What is your most treasured memory?"). The final question set moves to the most self-revealing disclosures (e.g., "If you were to die this evening with no opportunity to communicate with anyone, what would you most regret not having told someone?").

It doesn't take much time or effort to leverage self-disclosure in service to building relationship quality. Arrive at the Zoom room a few minutes early and chat with others who are there rather than staring at everyone else staring at their screens. When someone asks, "How are you?" or "How's your day going?," resist the urge to give the same old answer of "Good! Good! How about you?" Instead, give them an honest answer with a bit of detail ("I'm feeling on top of the world at the moment, I just signed a big client I've been hoping to work with for months!"). During the meeting,

---

[39] Laurenceau, J.-P., Barrett, L. F., & Pietromonaco, P. R. (1998). Intimacy as an interpersonal process: The importance of self-disclosure, partner disclosure, and perceived partner responsiveness in interpersonal exchanges. *Journal of Personality and Social Psychology, 74*(5), 1238–1251. https://doi.org/10.1037/0022-3514.74.5.1238

preface your comments about an agenda item with a brief disclosure about how you're feeling ("We've been struggling to find a solution to this challenge, so I'm both thrilled to finally be able to offer an option and also a bit nervous it may not work within our time constraints"). When drafting an email to a colleague, take the extra 20 seconds to give a quick personal update ("Have a great weekend, Jeff. I personally am looking forward to collapsing on the couch tonight with my friends Ben and Jerry. It's been a tough week.")

While self-disclosure itself helps drive closeness, perceiving that others are responsive to our disclosures is powerful, too. Thus, when a colleague shares something with you, acknowledge it with care and sincerity.

It's not useful to hear someone parrot back to you, "You said your computer crashed and that you are upset. Is that correct? If yes, press 1." A better response would be, "Oh wow. That's a big deal, especially knowing how carefully you craft every argument you make in your writing." Or, to the colleague who shared on Friday that it had been a tough week, you might drop a quick note Monday that says, "Just a quick note to say I hope the weekend brought you the R&R you needed after last week's challenges."

As an interpersonal process, self-disclosure provides a vehicle for creating connection, building trust, and exploring possibilities. Taking the risk of revealing one's true self, and having that self be seen and understood, enhances collaborative relationship quality.

Cultivate we-ness

Mutuality, or the psychological sense of sharing a social identity with another person, is a distinguishing feature of close relationships.

Researchers often talk about mutuality in terms of "inclusion of others in the self," which can be measured using the aptly named

Inclusion of Other in Self Scale.[40] The scale contains a series of seven pairs of overlapping circles, like the pair shown here. Each pair of circles overlaps slightly more than the preceding pair. The first pair of circles barely touch, whereas the final pair of circles are almost entirely overlapped. In research, we simply ask participants to pick the pair of circles that best describes their relationship with another person. If you were to draw a pair of circles to describe your relationship with your collaborator, how much overlap would there be?

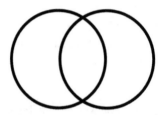

OVERLAPPING CIRCLES REPRESENT WE-NESS

In relationships with a high degree of we-ness, the line between self and other blurs. Other people, especially close others, inform who we are, enhance the tools we believe we have at our disposal, and shape how we see the world. A higher sense of mutuality is also associated with a higher willingness to share resources.

A nonprofit executive shared that this mutuality is key to what it means to collaborate. She asked, "Are we really in this together? In a moment of change or difficulty, am I going to prioritize my commitment to the collaboration or my individual response? If you and I are in a snowstorm driving on the highway, do we work together to get home safely, or do I leave you at the next rest stop and tell you to figure out your own way home?"

---

[40] Aron, A., Aron, E. N., & Smollan, D. (1992). Inclusion of other in the self scale and the structure of interpersonal closeness. *Journal of Personality and Social Psychology, 63*(4), 596-612. https://doi.org/10.1037/0022-3514.63.4.596

Turning for a moment to the close relationships research, romantic partners with higher levels of we-ness respond more constructively to relationship conflict; they express higher levels of commitment to the relationship, perceive their partners more positively, and are more satisfied with their relationships.[41] And, I love this fun fact: They use a higher proportion of plural pronouns ("we" did this versus "I" did this).[42]

While it is possible to lose oneself in a relationship, that risk seems low in most workplaces. Thus, in service to the positive functioning of your workplace collaborations, it's worth looking at the presence of we-ness on the team and perhaps nudging it along a bit in service to increasing relationship quality.

We already talked about one driver of we-ness: self-disclosure. Mutual self-disclosure has been shown to increase the inclusion of other in self. Other drivers of we-ness include sharing novel activities, humor, and perspective taking.[43] So, in the workplace, we might do things like take a challenging short course together, try a new place for lunch, pass around a funny meme (workplace appropriate!), call back a funny moment from a previous meeting, or simply ask "How do you see it?"

Seek novelty and challenge

The self-expansion model proposes that individuals are powerfully motivated to increase their agency in the world, making it

[41] Aron, A., Lewandowski, G., Branand, B., Mashek, D., & Aron, E. (2022). Self-expansion motivation and inclusion of others in self: An updated review. *Journal of Social and Personal Relationships*. https://doi. org/10.1177/02654075221110630

[42] Agnew, C. R., Van Lange, P. A., Rusbult, C. E., & Langston, C. A. (1998). Cognitive interdependence: Commitment and the mental representation of close relationships. *Journal of Personality and Social Psychology*, *74*(4), 939–954. https://doi.org/10.1037/0022-3514.74.4.939

[43] (Aron et al., 2022)

more likely that they will reach their future goals.[44] A feature of our human condition is that we want to be able to do, to be, and to create. That agency requires that we seek out—and gain access to—new resources such as knowledge, perspectives, identities, skills, and social networks.

One way we do so is through our relationships. When a relationship brings with it new resources, perspectives, or identities, that relationship creates self-expansion. And self-expansion is yet another driver of relationship quality.

Research by Gary Lewandowski and his colleagues[45] shows that people who report being in more self-expanding relationships are more satisfied in those relationships. They are also happier, more committed, more forgiving, and more willing to make room in the relationship for the other person's interests.

People who engage in novel and interesting pursuits experience self-expansion. In your personal life, these can be individual pursuits such as taking a ceramics class at the local art studio, couple pursuits such as joining a book club together, or your family taking on a community service project.

In your professional life, the individual pursuits might include taking a professional development course. The team pursuits might include attending a conference together or saying yes to a challenging new project.

However, if a novel pursuit is too challenging, exceeding available skill or capacity, stress can ensue, a state I call hyperexpansion. This insight is important when it comes to workplace collaboration because, as Timothy Knoster and colleagues point out, organizational change hits predictable snags when key ingredients

---

[44] (Aron et al., 2022)

[45] For an overview, see Aron et al., 2022.

are missing.[46] For example, anxiety kicks in when needed skills are absent and frustration mounts when needed resources are absent.[47] Asking a team to move mountains with a small crowbar doesn't create self-expansion, it creates stress.

Relationships that afford insufficient self-expansion are experienced as boring. The last thing you want in a collaborative relationship, or in any aspect of the workplace, is for people to be bored. When people are bored, they search for alternatives to their current situation.

In fact, we are drawn to relationships and experiences that we believe will provide self-expansion. Herein lies one of the many arguments for collaborating with diverse others. Dissimilar others introduce new perspectives, introduce us to new skills, and help us learn new things; they thus contribute to our self-expansion.

In a nutshell, novelty and challenge bode well for the quality of your collaborative relationships. So how might you harness this insight in service to your collaboration? Here are eight suggestions:

- Seek out and collaborate with diverse others.
- Seek out professional development opportunities to increase your agency in the workplace and beyond.
- Encourage your collaborators to do the same.
- Communicate your explicit support for collaborators who do so.
- When deciding roles and responsibilities for a given project, don't get into a rut; encourage yourself and others to take on new roles.

---

[46] Knoster, T., Villa, R., & Thousand, J. (2000). A framework for thinking about systems change. In R. Villa & J. Thousands (Eds.), *Restructuring for caring and effective education: Piecing the puzzle together* (2nd ed, pp. 93–128). Paul H. Brookes.

[47] I have summarized the Knoster et al. framework in a handout available in the Other Links section of www.collaborhate.com.

- Do novel things together as a team. This might be as simple as going to a new lunch spot or as complex as developing a new offering or product for your organization.
- Monitor for reliable access to the skills and resources needed to do the work well. If those are absent, explore options for bringing on more capacity to prevent stressful hyperexpansion.
- Be on the lookout for expressions of boredom in yourself and others. If they kick up, identify opportunities like those above to generate more positive self-expansion.

✖ Here's the point

- As one of the underlying dimensions of the Mashek Matrix, it's important to invest time and resources in improving collaborative relationship quality.
- Two modes of being—personality and attachment orientation—inform how we engage and experience collaborative relationships in the workplace.
- This chapter offers nine empirically informed strategies for improving collaborative relationship quality.

5 Take 5

1. What strategies from this chapter does your team already utilize? And in what ways do you think those strategies have affected your team's collaborative relationship quality?
2. How, if at all, has your or others' personality—especially agreeableness, conscientiousness, and emotional stability—played out in your collaborations ?
3. How, if at all, has your or others' attachment orientation played out in your collaborations?
4. Of the ideas shared in this chapter for improving collaborative relationship quality, which ideas do you

think might best fit your current situation? What features of the interpersonal, political, or resource environment lead you to this conclusion?

5. Thinking back over the history of your relationships with your collaborators, what role have you played in supporting or perhaps undermining collaborative relationship quality?

Chapter 4
Understanding interdependence

WHILE THE LAST chapter focused exclusively on the relationship quality dimension of the Mashek Matrix, this chapter focuses on interdependence, the second dimension of the Matrix.

Interdependence exists when each person's outcomes are influenced by the other person's behaviors. In this chapter, I first unpack key ideas about the outcomes that sit at the heart of interdependence. Then, I introduce ten strategies for shifting interdependence in your collaborative relationships.

> *Interdependence exists when each person's outcomes are influenced by the other's behavior.*

Let's consider: Outcomes

What are outcomes?

Interdependence theory[48] was one of my favorite topics to teach in my *Psychology of Close Relationships* courses at Harvey Mudd College. The students there are incredibly smart and mathematically gifted. They'd laugh—OK, they'd *sometimes* laugh—when I'd say that we can apply their math wizardry to understand relationship functioning. I'd then write this very simple equation on the board:

Outcomes = Rewards - Costs

Rewards are anything you personally find desirable. For example, in a collaborative relationship, rewards might include things like access to a new network of contacts, know-how that moves the project along, or the belly laughs that ensue when your collaborator impersonates a turtle.

Costs, on the other hand, are anything you find aversive or undesirable. In your collaborative relationships, costs can be anything from the embarrassment you feel when your collaborator asks a client an inappropriate question, guilt when you drop a ball that impacts your collaborator's work, stress when a slipped timeline impacts your weekend plans, or the nuisance of having to add yet another standing meeting to your calendar.

According to interdependence theory, we're all looking for the best outcomes possible in our relationships and in our interactions. We seek to maximize rewards and minimize costs.[49] For now, the important thing to remember is that, in interdependent

---

[48] Kelley, H. H., & Thibaut, J. W. (1978). *Interpersonal relations: A theory of interdependence.* Wiley.

[49] The strategies covered in Chapter 3 play a role in improving our collaborators' outcomes.

relationships, individuals reciprocally influence each other's outcomes.

What's fair?

According to interdependence theory, we're all looking for the best outcomes possible in our relationships and in our interactions. We seek to maximize rewards and minimize costs.

In collaborations, like in all relationships, it's important to play fair. And fairness has a lot to do with outcomes. Keep in mind: we're all looking for the best outcomes possible in our relationships.

I'd venture to say we've all had the experience of being in a group where a collaborator shirks all responsibility or does shoddy work that needs to be redone by others. Such free-riders are the bane of a good collaborator's existence. It's incredibly annoying to be tethered in any way to someone who fails to contribute their fair share to the common good. In fact, social psychological research consistently demonstrates that we hate being under benefited.[50] But what exactly does that mean?

Imagine there exists a ratio for each person on the team, where one number represents that person's contributions and the other number represents that person's outcomes. "My" outcomes can include those communal outcomes we all receive—like recognition for the team's good work or the sense of helping the world by inventing a clever solution. And, the more overlap you see between yourself and your collaborator ("we-ness," see Chapter 3), the more likely you are to experience the other person's outcomes, to some extent, as your outcomes (that is, we bask in the reflected glory of those we are close to). So this imagined ratio

---

[50] Hatfield, E., & Rapson, R. L. (2012). Equity theory in close relationships. In P. Van Lange, A. Kruglanski, & E. T. Higgins (Eds.), *Handbook of theories in social psychology* (Vol. 2, pp. 200–217). Sage.

of contributions and outcomes includes all these possible types of outcomes.

According to equity theorists, we don't necessarily need to be putting in equal contributions or benefiting with equal outcomes. Instead, we need the *proportion*—the ratio of outcomes to contributions—to be equal. Relationships feel balanced when one person's ratio equals the other person's ratio.

Let's make this fascinating point salient with an example. Imagine you and a colleague are co-authoring a report that is sure to make waves in the industry once it's released. You are both putting in your best work on this report and you're going to share the accolades and positive attention that's soon to come your way.

> *According to equity theorists, we don't necessarily need to be putting in equal contributions or benefiting with equal outcomes. Instead, we need the proportion—the ratio of outcomes to benefits—to be equal.*

Your outcome: Your contribution = 100:100 = 1

Your colleague's outcome: Your colleague's contribution = 100:100 = 1

Your ratios are even. This is an equitable, or fair, relationship.

Now, what if your colleague is only doing, say, half the work you're doing? According to equity theory, this relationship is still equitable provided their outcomes are also halved. For example, your colleague, although named as an author, will be in the second-author position and won't be taking part in the media roll out of the report (thus, you will get the limelight—let's imagine for a moment that this is something you personally value).

The ratios might look something like this:

Your outcome: Your contribution = 100:100 = 1

Your colleague's outcome: Your colleague's contribution = 50:50 = 1

This is still a fair or equitable relationship.

But what happens when the ratios fall out of equivalency? For example, you're busting your butt on this report, but your co-author, who happens to be in a more senior role and will get first authorship and the accolades, is distracted with other commitments and seems only able to give this report cursory consideration on an intermittent basis.

The ratios might look something like this:

Your outcome: Your contribution = 25:100 = .25

Your colleague's outcome: Your colleague's contribution = 100:25 = 4

Uh oh. Now we have an imbalance. Your ratio of .25 is paltry compared to your collaborator's 4. In this case, you are wildly under benefited and your collaborator is over benefited.

And, guess what? When we're feeling the sting of being under benefited, we are more likely to track contributions and outcomes. That is, when interacting with takers, there's a tendency to move into exchange rather than communal ways of being (we talked about exchange versus communal norms in Chapter 3). It's harder to muster enthusiasm for the communal good when you feel like a collaborator is taking advantage of you.

So how do you restore equity? There are four options: change your contributions, change your outcomes, change your collaborator's contributions, or change your collaborator's outcomes.

Ideally, these changes occur through explicit conversation and expectation setting as opposed to, for example, you just stopping doing the work. (Shhh... someone is quietly quitting). If you're being under benefited, for example, you could say to your collaborator: "I'm pouring my heart and soul into this report, and I can see what a positive contribution I'm making. I'd like to discuss options for making my role publicly visible in the final roll out."

There's the chance, of course, that you are the one being over benefited in a collaboration. Raise this possibility with your collaborator so that you can work to re-establish equity. You might say, "Hey, it feels to me like you're doing more than your fair share of the work on this project. Can we talk about how to even that out or, perhaps, how to make sure you'll get the credit you deserve when it comes time to roll this out?"

One important caveat to hold in mind when assessing equity is that we are generally quite clear about our own contributions to shared work. Our work on a project is salient to us. Afterall, we were there. But, others' work is often invisible to us. It's harder for us to see, track, and remember. In a classic study on this effect, psychologists Michael Ross and Fiore Sicoly asked married couples to independently estimate the percentage of household chores they completed.[51] Then the estimates of the individuals within each couple were summed. Guess what? For 27 of the 37 couples, the sum exceeded 100%, meaning that at least one person in 73% of the couples showed this tendency to over estimate one's own contributions.

The caution then is this: just because you're feeling under benefited doesn't mean you truly are getting a raw deal. You may be missing at least part of the picture, so try to truly see your collaborator's contributions. Brainstorm with your collaborator ways you can both make your work visible, thank others for the behind-the-scenes legwork they're doing, and celebrate each other's contributions. Talk to your collaborator about your sense and invite a conversation to level set on contributions and outcomes.

A second caveat is that, just as there are free-riders, there are also those who take a "my way or the highway" approach to shared

[51] Ross, M., & Sicoly, F. (1979). Egocentric biases in availability and attribution. *Journal of Personality and Social Psychology, 37*(3), 322–336. https://doi.org/10.1037/0022-3514.37.3.322

work. In fact, they might not allow any space at all for your ideas, your know-how, or your talents. This is a huge problem, not least because it doesn't even qualify as collaboration. These rogue "collaborators" may be under the misperception that they're the one doing everyone else a big favor. I'd like to go on record right now: they are not. Unilaterally imposing one's ideas and approach on a collaboration doesn't count as carrying the load. Instead, it completely undermines the work and creates outcomes for others they simply aren't choosing. Framing the impact of this rogue behavior in terms of respective outcomes and contributions may help alleviate the behavior.

A third and final caveat concerns power. The principle of least interest, first proposed by sociologist Willard Waller in 1938,[52] says that, in a relationship, the person with the least interest in the relationship has the most power. If there's an asymmetry to the extent you and your collaborator need or want this collaboration, the person who could most easily walk away has more say and sway in the relationship. As Elijah Wee and colleagues conclude in a fascinating paper about abusive supervision in the workplace, "only when the follower is asymmetrically dependent on the leader for goals and resources is the leader significantly more powerful than the follower, and therefore more likely to exploit and abuse the follower."[53]

Three dials for influencing outcomes and thus altering interdependence

As I touched on in Chapter 2, researchers who study interdependence focus on three observable patterns of interaction

[52] Waller, W. (1938). The family: A dynamic interpretation. Cordon Company.
[53] Wee, E. X. M., Liao, H., Liu, D., & Liu, J. (2017). Moving from abuse to reconciliation: A power-dependence perspective on when and how a follower can break the spiral of abuse. Academy of Management Journal, 60(6), 2352–2380. https://doi.org/10.5465/amj.2015.0866

when trying to characterize how interdependent a relationship is: frequency, diversity, and strength.[54]

- **Frequency** concerns the amount of time spent together. The more frequently you interact with a collaborator, the more opportunities there are to influence each other's outcomes and thus the more interdependent the relationship.
- **Diversity** refers to the range of activities you engage in with your collaborator. The more diverse the set of activities you engage in together, the broader the range of outcomes that could be influenced and thus the more interdependent your relationship.
- **Strength** concerns the degree of influence you and your collaborator have on each other's behaviors, decisions, plans, goals, accomplishments, and so on. If you and your collaborator have significant sway over these outcomes, then the relationship is more interdependent than one in which you can't rock each other's boats no matter how hard you might try.

You may have noticed that all the strategies offered in Chapter 3 intend to *improve* relationship quality. That's because, while you might be in a situation where you need to take your foot off the gas in terms of increasing relationship quality, there's unlikely to ever be a scenario in which you'd want to intentionally reduce relationship quality with a collaborator.

The same isn't true of interdependence. Each of these facets—frequency, diversity, and strength—is a dial that can be adjusted to increase *or* decrease interdependence. This is important because, to move from collabor(h)ate to collaborGREAT, you will need to adjust interdependence both up and down. We'll

---

[54] (Berscheid et al., 2004)

talk in Chapter 5 about the situations in which those different strategies will be needed.

Four strategies to turn the frequency dial

The potential for interdependence increases as you spend more time with your collaborator. Adjusting the frequency dial, then, involves scaling up or scaling back interaction time. Recognizing that you may not have the ability or authority to make all of these changes within your workplace, here are four strategies to consider.

Change formal time together

Some organizations' meeting rhythms are so entrenched that nobody knows their origin. Others are more dynamic, changing as the needs of the people and projects change. If your colleagues might be amenable to changing the meeting rhythm, you can increase interdependence by suggesting something like, "A second short meeting each week would help keep the forward momentum. Are others open to that?" Or, conversely, you can decrease interdependence with, "Would others be open to stepping back to an every-other-week meeting cadence? It seems we're covering the same ground each week because there's not enough time between meetings to make progress on our tasks." If you and your collaborator tend to work side-by-side, you can also increase or decrease how often that side-by-side work happens to, respectively, increase or decrease interdependence.

Change informal time together

Options for creating more informal time include asking a colleague if they'd like to join you for a "walk and talk" (which you can do either in-person or over the phone), grabbing coffee or lunch together (again, in-person or virtually), or simply stopping by someone's desk or direct messaging them to ask for an impromptu brainstorming session. Moves like these can increase interdependence by amping up the frequency with which influence can unfold.

Conversely, reducing informal interaction time can help decrease interdependence. Depending on your organization's policies and norms, you can hold "do not disturb" times on your calendar, place a little cube on your desk like those they use in Brazilian barbeque restaurants to signal whether you're open to being interrupted,[55] or talk to your colleague to reset a boundary. You can kick off such a boundary-reset conversation by saying: "I enjoy working on our project, but I also need to focus at times on my other work. I suggest we keep a running document of questions and issues we'd like to discuss but hold actual discussion of those things until our scheduled meetings. This would really help me focus. Does this plan work for you?"

Change how much headspace you share

Ruminations about negative events can follow us home, intrude on our family time, keep us up at night, and otherwise hijack our thoughts. If you find yourself ruminating on something your colleague said or did (or didn't say or do), you're spending psychological time with them. Even in their absence, the collaborator is exerting influence with some frequency and thus increasing interdependence.

To reduce rumination, try:

- Dumping your thoughts into a journal for five minutes as part of your workday shutdown ritual.

---

[55] My son made me one of these when we were both working from the kitchen table during COVID; it worked like a charm.

- Starting a simple mindfulness practice (there are a lot of apps and websites that offer on-demand recordings to help you on your way to the Zen garden).
- Exercising to blow off steam.
- Taking a time-limited (e.g., 30 minutes) deep dive into the issue to identify the core need or fear that's behind the worry, then identify a single step you can take tomorrow to help address the situation.

Conversely, you can also increase the headspace you give to a collaborator to increase interdependence. Two examples include:

- Reflecting on what you are grateful for about your collaborator (e.g., they gave you a reassuring look during your presentation, they cracked a joke that made you smile, they caught a typo before you sent the email to the whole company).
- Engaging in a little relationship strategic planning. Ask yourself: In what ways am I contributing to positive versus negative outcomes for my collaborator? What am I doing well in our collaboration that I can continue? What am I not doing well that I can discontinue or change? What are three steps I can take yet this week to advance that change?

Change expectations about response time

Zooming out for a moment, recall that these strategies for altering time together seek to adjust the frequency with which collaborators impact each other. That's an important reminder as we consider this final recommendation: change expectations about response time.

As leadership researcher Rob Cross points out in his book *Beyond collaboration overload,*[56] one way we hamstring our and our colleagues' ability to get any real work done is we expect each other to be hyperconnected, available, and responsive throughout the day… and night… and on weekends. Technology, of course fuels that insatiable fire.

You risk receiving intrusive notifications from many different applications as triggered by many different collaborators around the clock. The frequency with which collaborators can impact each other skyrockets with the combination of technology and the expectation of responsiveness. This is collaboration overload.

To help protect yourself and others from collaboration overload, you'll want to decrease interdependence by loosening expectations around hyper availability and responsiveness. To that end, Cross offers a wonderful range of solutions, including:

> *The frequency with which collaborators can impact each other skyrockets with the combination of technology and the expectation of responsiveness.*

- Setting expectations (see Chapter 3 for guidelines on that front).
- Co-creating solutions (given many people face challenges on this front, you'll likely find others are eager to find solutions).
- Establishing routines around when and how to respond to requests for help.

On the flip side, you can also increase interdependence by ratcheting up expectations around responsiveness. For example, it would be appropriate, likely within the expectation-setting

[56] Cross, R. (2021). *Beyond collaboration overload.* Harvard Business Review Press.

conversations discussed in Chapter 3, to set a team standard around things like response times and response windows. Then, if someone takes a week to reply to urgent emails when you all had agreed to a 24-hour reply within the work week, you have firm ground for a tactful accountability conversation.

One strategy to turn the diversity dial

More interdependence is also possible when you engage in an increasingly diverse range of activities with your collaborator. For example, if you and Hannah stage the newsletter once per month, but you don't really do much else together, then Hannah's ability to influence you is contained. If, on the other hand, the two of you each play a role in designing, coordinating, and launching all external-facing communications and you're on the same hiring committee and your kids are in the same Girl Scout troop, then there's a higher potential for more interdependence. (And if the troop leader asks the two of you to co-lead the cookie sales this year, then you're in for some extra interdependent fun.)

Do more or less together

Conceptually, it seems straightforward to change the range of activities you're involved in with your collaborator. Do fewer types of things together to decrease interdependence and do more types of things together to increase it. Simple enough, right?

Not exactly. While standing meetings, regimented processes, precise position descriptions, and documented policies each play a valuable role in creating visible and (hopefully) navigable pathways to and through work, they can also make it difficult to adjust activities on the fly or in a temporary way to alter the range of activities you and a collaborator are involved in.

Within the context of all those constraints, finding ways to do less together (and thereby decreasing interdependence) can be especially challenging. The work still needs to get done. And individuals put their jobs at risk if they unilaterally decide to just stop doing chunks of their assigned work. Decreasing the range of activities, then, may not be available to you in all situations.

That said, it may be possible to approach managers with requests like:

- "To protect time for Priority Project A, I'd like to back-burner Project H for the remainder of this quarter."
- "Collaborating on Project A instead of B would give me a stretch opportunity to demonstrate I'm ready for the next role up."

Managers would be wise to explore the needs behind such requests, including probing for the possibility of collaborator challenges that could be improved with less interdependence.

In a lot of workplaces, it is easier to increase the range of activities engaged in with a collaborator. These requests can be pitched as:

- "We're ready to take on new challenges for the organization."
- "Taking up X role on Y project would help me put recent training into practice and cement that new learning."

Five strategies to turn the strength dial

Let's now consider the strength of influence collaborators can have on each other's outcomes, behaviors, decisions, plans, and goals. Researchers who study workplace teams are generally interested in two aspects of strength of influence: how work is structured[57]

---

[57] Organizational researchers call this *task interdependence*; for the sake of clarity, I do not use this label in the text to avoid confusion with relationship interdependence.

and how work is measured and rewarded.[58] [59] These two aspects of strength of influence give rise to five strategies for adjusting interdependence within collaborative relationships; the first two strategies focus on how work is structured and the last three focus on how work is measured and rewarded.

Change how workflows are structured

Work can be designed so that collaborators must rely on one another for access to critical resources and so that completion of the work requires coordinated action.[60]

Most teamwork is coordinated in one of three ways.[61] Work can be done individually and then pooled together to form a final product. This is the standard "divide and conquer" approach many students rely on to complete work—you write the introduction, I'll write the methods, Sam will take the results. A pooled approach like this, in which the work of individuals is added together to create the whole, ranks low on interdependence.

A step up from there is sequential interdependence where individuals touch the project in a known, linear order such that each person can add to or make use of what already exists. Imagine a content creation team where Person A works with the division lead to draft and approve copy. Person A hands off the final copy

---

[58] Organizational researchers call this *outcome interdependence*; for the sake of clarity, I do not use this label in the text to avoid confusion with both relationship interdependence and outcomes.

[59] Courtright, S. H., Thurgood, G. R., Stewart, G. L., & Pierotti, A. J. (2015). Structural interdependence in teams: An integrative framework and meta-analysis. *Journal of Applied Psychology, 100*(6), 1825–1846. https://doi.org/10.1037/apl0000027

[60] (Courtright et al., 2015)

[61] Thompson, J. D. (1967). *Organizations in action: Social science bases of administrative theory.* McGraw-Hill.

to Person B who identifies images from the company's archive for the website. And Person C then takes those inputs to draft a webpage, which then gets shared back with the division lead for approval. Waterfall project management relies on sequential handoffs like these.

A step up from there is reciprocal interdependence, which is iterative, flexible, and agile (unsurprisingly, agile project management methodologies bake in reciprocal interdependence). For example, on the conference planning team the program chair defines the theme and provides an initial list of dream speakers. The copywriter prepares some preliminary marketing text, seeking input from the program chair along the way before sending it to the program assistants so they can begin extending speaker invites. As the acceptances start rolling in, the copywriter updates the marketing text to reflect the exciting line up. Eventually, the communications team puts together a draft program, which then has to be modified because Famous Speaker A just had to drop out. But, no fear, the program assistants were able to find someone to fill that slot, but she's only going to be able to speak at 9am, so that's going to require we shift the coffee break back 30 minutes. The take home point is that there are a lot of moving parts and feedback loops in reciprocal, intensive workflows. As such they are highly interdependent.

A word of caution is warranted here: sequential or reciprocal interdependence needn't equal cumbersome bureaucracies. Granted, in some larger organizations, workflows can become comically complex. The purchase order can't be processed until Jake in legal confirms that the modification to subclause II.3.a.i requested by Anne in purchasing fully aligns with this year's policy handbook, because there was a new addition that the committee voted in last quarter. Such complexity, especially when it exists within a culture of sluggish or incomplete communications, renders action nearly impossible.

But organization size doesn't necessarily have to create cumbersome workflows. One tech leader from a large social media company (yes, you've heard of them, but I'm unable to use the name here) observed that quick feedback loops on ideas and implementations is a hallmark of the company culture. "It's like watching a huge giant do graceful ballet, quite frankly. It's really impressive," he observed.

Change how resources are accessed

Sometimes collaborators must rely on each other to access project-critical resources. If only one person has the know-how to knock out a particular task, or if all outreach to an external partner must flow through a single point of contact, or if one person is the sole decider on all budgetary issues, dependence is high. I deliberately chose the word dependence here, rather than interdependence because interdependence assumes mutual dependence.

The process by which perspectives, information, know-how, and other resources are summoned, allocated, monitored, and managed are all elements that could potentially drive interdependence. The degree to which my work depends on your willingness and ability to summon appropriate resources at the right time informs the degree to which I feel my wagon is hitched to your horse. And vice versa.

Let's turn now to the second aspect of strength of influence: how work is measured and rewarded. Work can be "measured, rewarded, and communicated at the group level so as to emphasize collective outputs rather than individual contributions."[62] Here are three strategies for moving between group-level and individual-level measurements and rewards.

---

[62] (Courtright et al., 2015)

Change how goals are specified

Goals can be specified at the level of the individual contributor or the level of the group. Imagine a fundraising team at a nonprofit has the goal to raise $10 million from new donors this year. The development manager has a choice to make here. She could specify that each of five team members is expected to independently raise $2 million; this is an example of an individual-level goal. Or, she could specify that the team as a whole is expected to raise $10 million; this is an example of a group-level goal. Group-level goals strengthen interdependence, whereas individual-level goals weaken it.

Change how progress toward goals is tracked

Progress toward goals can be tracked at either the individual level or the group level. The fundraising team's metrics dashboard, for example, could display everyone's money raised and then provide a roll-up for the team's overall statistics. Or the dashboard could display just the individual amounts or just the team amount. Providing individual data, even in combination with group-level data, signals that the work of individuals is valued at least on par with the work of the team. As such, it weakens interdependence. On the other hand, tracking only team-level metrics strengthens everyone's influence on each other ("I" can't make progress unless "we" make progress) and thus promotes interdependence.

Change how rewards and costs are allocated

Success and failure can also be based on individual-level or group-level performance. If our fundraising team meets the group-level goal, everyone on the team might get the same bonus, for example. That approach to rewarding work promotes interdependence because one person's outcomes are strongly influenced by others on the team. Alternatively, individuals could receive an allocation of the bonus pool based on the proportion of the funds they individually raised. That approach decreases interdependence and sets up internal competition.

Sometimes, co-workers influence rewards in another way: they may be invited to provide input on each other's performance and that input may inform salary increases. I'm flashing back to my professor days here; in particular, the challenge of structuring effective group work. In an effort to prevent free-riders from receiving a high grade if in fact they had done squat to contribute to the group's work, I'd ask each person on the team to evaluate the quality of the contributions made by each other member of the team at multiple points during the semester. I would then factor in any variance into that individual's grade, which would be separate from the overall grade given to the specific product created by the group.[63]

Similar peer performance reviews exist in the workplace. These primarily take the form of "cheers" or "high fives," expressions of gratitude for the positive contributions someone has made to your work or experience at work. The more these peer performance reviews figure into valued downstream outcomes (such as compensation), the stronger the influence on outcomes and thus more interdependence they drive.

There are other rewards that accrue that we may not at first think about because they exist outside the formal channels. For example, a collaborator can shape others' opinions of you, help or hurt your access to professional networks, increase or decrease the likelihood you'll be invited to prestigious events, or increase or

---

[63] One college professor I know tries to protect against the students having a miserable groupwork experience by giving an ungraded assignment early in the semester. He uses the thoroughness of students' responses as a proxy for their conscientiousness. Later, he uses that variable to surreptitiously assign students to groups such that those who did a good job completing the ungraded assignment work together and those who phoned it in get stuck with each other.

decrease the likelihood you will be considered for a valued opportunity to present your team's work to the client. Thus, when thinking about ways to increase or decrease strength of influence, think beyond the formal structures of work.

Before closing this section, it's important to note that, ideally, how work is structured aligns with how work will be measured and rewarded. If you say you'd like your team to be highly interdependent, make sure to structure both tasks and outcomes accordingly. If you claim that you want everyone pitching in to create a stone soup,[64] but then reward individual performance, you're creating a disincentive for people to play nice. As teachers, parents, and pet owners know all too well: What gets rewarded gets repeated.

Here's the point

- According to interdependence theory, we're all looking for the best outcomes possible in our relationships and in our interactions.
- Collaborators are happiest in relationships where individuals' outcomes-to-contributions proportions are equitable.
- Collaborative relationships exhibit high interdependence when there is a high frequency of impact across a diverse range of activities and when the influence is strong.
- Altering time together, range of activities, and how work is structured, measured, and rewarded changes the level of interdependence within a collaborative relationship; these changes can be achieved by turning the frequency, diversity, and strength dials.

---

[64] Stone soup is a folk tale in which villagers each contribute an ingredient to create a tasty soup that far surpassed what any of them could have made by themselves.

�❺ Take 5

1. In light of the claim that we are all trying to optimize our outcomes in our collaborative relationships, what benefits do you especially value? And what costs do you find especially weighty? How do your responses line up with those of your collaborators? And how might the degree of alignment inform decisions about how to structure or reward shared work?

2. Have you ever felt under benefited or over benefited in a collaborative relationship? How did it feel? How aware of your experience was your collaborator and did they see the situation similarly? What steps, if any, did you take to re-establish balance?

3. If you have multiple collaborators on a given project, what do you notice about your degree of interdependence with each person? In what ways is your interdependence with one person influenced by your interdependence with the other(s)?

4. What ideas from this chapter do your team already consider in its work? In what ways do you think this awareness has affected your team's interdependence, happiness, and effectiveness?

5. Given the political, cultural, and resource realities of your particular workplace, which of the suggested pathways for altering interdependence seem most viable?

Chapter 5
A DIY workshop: Leveraging the Mashek Matrix to improve your collaborative relationships

In Chapter 2, you learned about the two dimensions of the Mashek Matrix: relationship quality and interdependence. In Chapter 3, you learned research-backed strategies to increase relationship quality. In Chapter 4 you learned how to adjust interdependence by altering factors at the heart of interdependence theory: the frequency, diversity, and strength of impact.

Now, with all these puzzle pieces on the table, let's put them together. In this chapter, I describe in detail a DIY self-guided workshop for applying these ideas to enhance your collaborative relationships. The big questions at hand are, assuming you'd like to move a relationship from collabor(h)ate to collaborGREAT, what should you do and when should you do it? The answers may surprise you.

Before diving into the workshop, I'd like to call your attention to two resources to help along the way.

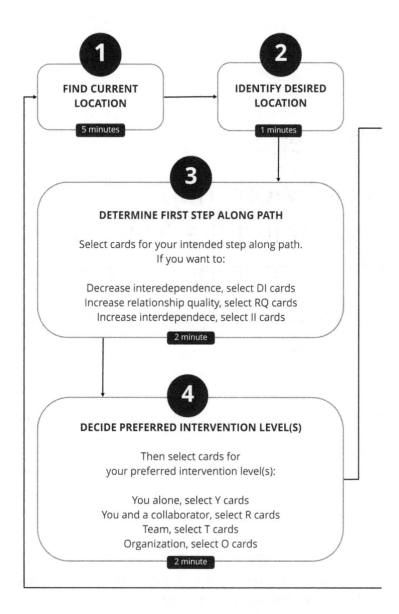

VISUAL OVERVIEW OF THE DIY WORKSHOP

5

BRAINSTORM SPECIFIC IDEAS

Brainstorm specific ideas for bringing each strategy to life; generate as many ideas as possible.

`30 minutes`

6

SYSTEMATICALLY EVALUATE OPTIONS

A.
Remove any cards that are not resonant with organizational values or your values

B.
Rate each card on three qualities: Feasbility, Desirability, Viability

C.
Remove any cards that received a 0 or 1 on one or more qualities

D.
Array remaining cards from low to high

E.
Select the highest scoring idea; if multiple cards clustered at the top, select the idea you think is most interesting or exciting

`20 minutes`

7

PLAN AND IMPLEMENT
`Variable`

8

OBSERVE AND LEARN
`Variable`

9

NOW WHAT?
`Variable`

First, the flowchart provides a visual overview of the workshop. Individuals generally move through Steps 1–6 in about 60 minutes. If you're working through these steps with one or more collaborators, you will want to allow more time to ensure everyone's ideas are being heard and considered. You are, of course, welcome to skip or change steps that don't make sense within your context.

Second, there's a card deck waiting for you in the Digital downloads section of www.collaborhate.com. You'll be interacting with these cards in Steps 3–6, so you may want to print them now.

Finally, a word of encouragement: I share here the full protocol I use with clients looking to identify viable pathways for improving collaborative relationships. While my presenting it as a regimented set of steps means you'll be able to make it your own, it also risks making this whole relationship improvement thing feel quite rigid and tedious. Take heart. Please play around. Take as many passes as you like through these steps. Skip some. Add others. Try it once over coffee and once over cocktails. Experiment. Observe. Fail. Have fun.

Step 1: Find current location

To get to where you want to be, first figure out where you are. When it comes to locating yourself within the Mashek Matrix, you have two options.

First, you can work from intuition. Returning to the high-level conceptual definitions of both relationship quality and interdependence, ask yourself if your collaborative relationship is relatively high or low on each dimension, then simply select the quadrant in the Matrix that you think best captures where you are now. The intuitive approach offers a reasonable enough gut check on the fly, especially for the relationship quality dimension.

Second, you can work from psychological measurement. Building on the empirical research of a multitude of psychologists who study close relationships and organizations, I developed a self-report assessment that can be used by individuals to locate a particular relationship within the Matrix. If you haven't already completed the Collaborative Relationship Assessment, I encourage you to go to the Digital download section of www.collaborhate.com to do so.

The instrument will give you both a relationship quality score (labeled as "CRQ") and an interdependence score (labeled as "INT"). Use a solid dot to plot your current location on the graph below. I recommend writing the date you completed the assessment next to your dot so you will have both a time and location baseline to refer to for future reflection. Some people also find it useful to jot a brief description of what's going on right now in the relationship and at work to provide context for future reflection. For example, what's going particularly well or poorly in your collaborative relationship? What projects are you working on? These are details you may not remember a year from now when you look back on that little dot.

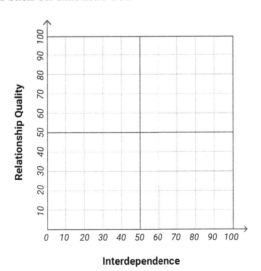

PLOT YOUR POSITION IN THE MATRIX

Step 2: Identify desired location

Next, do a little soul searching to determine your desired location in the matrix. While many of us would like to be at collaborGREAT,[65] be forewarned: it takes real effort to get there and stay there. Plot your desired location using a circle (rather than the dot, which you used to plot your current location). Again, note the date next to the circle and, if desired, leave some notes for your future self about why you'd like your relationship to move to this point.

Step 3: Determine first step along path

While the pathway to collaborGREAT involves adjusting both quality and interdependence, the order in which these adjustments take place depends on your starting quadrant. The previous two chapters talked about *how* to make those adjustments. In this section, we'll talk about the *order* of those adjustments. There's a bit of a twist here, so stick with me.

Take a look at the updated Matrix below. Notice the big barrier between collabor(h)ate and collaborGREAT? This barrier is like a really high, really thick brick wall. It's inordinately difficult to move any relationship directly from a place of "high interdependence and low quality" to a place of "high interdependence and high quality."

Why is that? Well, when a bunch of outcomes you care deeply about are tightly tethered to the behaviors of a collaborator *while* you're not feeling great about your relationship with that person,

---

[65] If your actual goal is something more akin to high potential, I get it. Just as we don't have room in our lives for 1,000 best friends, we also don't have room in our work lives for 1,000 collaborative relationships that are collaborGREAT. The process described in this chapter will still help, just stop once you get to where you want to be.

it's next to impossible to convince your head and heart to "just make things better." The risks are too salient.

Thus, when beginning in a state of collabor(h)ate, the first move should focus on decreasing interdependence, not increasing quality. This will feel counterintuitive to some readers.

There's an interesting parallel here to marital discord. Imagine a marriage in crisis. The two people are so fed up with each other that they think divorce is probably the way to go. They decide, finally, to seek couples' therapy. After a few sessions, they decide they're not quite ready to call it quits and decide the relationship is worth working on. They realize that's going to be next to impossible to do while living under the same roof where all the same triggers and dramas will keep playing out, despite their best intentions.

The couple decides that both people would benefit from a little breathing room and that the best first step is for one person to move out of the house, at least for a few months. This move decreases interdependence because, now, there are fewer opportunities for the people to impact each other's daily experience. Frequency, diversity, and strength of impact have all decreased. What's for dinner, the size of the laundry pile, the television volume, the kids' evening routine, the size of the grocery bill, the density of the social calendar, and so on are now totally up to each person. With more breathing room, they can then focus on improving their relationship quality. If and when they make it onto sturdier ground, they can move back in together; that is, after re-establishing relationship quality, than can re-establish interdependence.

The same dynamics exist for collaborative relationships in a state of collabor(h)ate. First figure out ways to decrease interdependence. Doing so provides the individuals with headspace and heart space to do the hard work of improving relationship quality.

The pathway from collabor(h)ate to collaborGREAT, then, flows clockwise through the model. You will need to navigate around the big brick wall that stands between collabor(h)ate and collaborGREAT by, first, *decreasing* interdependence, then increasing relationship quality, and then *increasing* interdependence.

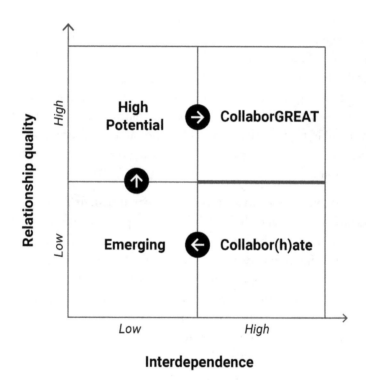

HOW TO MOVE THROUGH THE MASHEK MATRIX

If you're already in the high potential quadrant, you may want to work to increase interdependence. Keep in mind that you will also want to *maintain* relationship quality. If you're ramping up interdependence and relationship quality slips, you risk landing squarely in the zone of collabor(h)ate. Ignore relationship quality at your own peril.

If, when you plotted your location in the matrix, you found you were in the emerging quadrant, focus first on developing relationship quality, then on increasing interdependence.

Likewise, new relationships are generally in the emerging quadrant. They generally don't have much in place by way of either relationship quality or interdependence. If this describes your situation, you will likewise want to focus first on building relationship quality, then on building interdependence. Get to know—and like—each other first, then engage in increasingly more complicated and intertwined projects. Invest in relationship quality early on; the longer a new relationship sits in the emerging quadrant, the more likely interdependencies will pop up. Rather than having the relationship inadvertently slide backward toward collabor(h)ate, you'll want to nudge it toward collaborGREAT.

Finally, if you're one of the lucky ones already in the zone of collaborGREAT, high five! Keep on doing what you're doing, nurturing both relationship quality and interdependence. Like with any relationship, however, be careful not to rest on your laurels. Keep investing in the relationship and check in with your collaborator to ensure they're getting what they need from the relationship. After all, needs and preferences change. Take deliberate action to learn about and accommodate (or not) those shifts.

Critically, movement through the matrix is dynamic. Just as we wouldn't expect a married couple to always be happy—especially in the absence of persistent relationship maintenance work—we also shouldn't expect a collaborative relationship to achieve the desired state of collaborGREAT and then just miraculously hover there. The addition of a new collaborator or a new boss, a shift in the client's interests, a big challenge, an unexpected success, and so on can flip you into another quadrant. That's OK. That's expected. The trick is to recognize when a shift has happened and to mindfully engage in compensatory work to re-establish the desired state.

Be forewarned: While it is tough to go straight from collabor-(h)ate to collaborGREAT, the opposite isn't true. Imagine there's an uncovered manhole sitting atop that big brick wall between collaborGREAT and collabor(h)ate. A single major transgression within the collaboration could send you falling fast through the manhole. It's near impossible to shimmy back up without taking the long route home.

Before moving on to Step 4, make sure you're clear on your first move. Are you trying to:

- Decrease interdependence
- Increase relationship quality, or
- Increase interdependence?

Now, grab that card deck you printed out at the top of the chapter. Locate all the cards that include ideas for your first move. Ideas that can help decrease interdependency have DI in the top left corner. Those that can help increase relationship quality have an RQ. And those that can help increase interdependence have an II. Hold onto just those cards that contain ideas for your first move; you can set the others aside.

Step 4: Decide preferred level of intervention

You are an individual. I don't mean that in a "you're a one-of-a-kind, glorious, glitter-encrusted being" sort of way (though I have no doubt you are that, too). I mean it more in a "you are a person separate from others" way. In addition, you have relationships with each of your collaborators. In addition, some of those collaborative relationships likely exist within a given team. In addition, that team functions within an organization (or perhaps across organizations).

Like Russian nesting dolls, individuals are nested within relationships, relationships are nested within teams, and teams are nested within organizations. When looking to improve collaborative relationships, we can intervene at any or all these levels. And, because all are inter-connected, what we do at one level impacts other levels.

This means that, in your quest to transition your collaborative relationship from collabor(h)ate to collaborGREAT, there are a lot of different levers you could potentially pull. Some focus on you the individual, some focus on your relationship with one other person, some focus on the team, and some focus on your organization.

The previous two chapters offered strategies for decreasing interdependence (Chapter 4), increasing relationship quality (Chapter 3), and increasing interdependence (Chapter 4). The tables below list those strategies and indicates at which level each could potentially be applied.

Decrease interdependence	You	Relationship	Team	Organization
Decrease formal time together	●	●	●	●
Decrease informal time together	●	●	●	
Decrease amount of headspace you spend thinking about your collaborator	●			
Decrease expectations about responsiveness	●	●	●	●
Do fewer types of things together	●	●	●	
Decrease task interdependence by establishing pooled (or perhaps sequential) workflows		●	●	●
Loosen control of resources			●	●
Create individual-level goals			●	●
Track progress toward goals using individual-level metrics			●	●
Base rewards on individual-level performance			●	●

Increase relationship quality	You	Relationship	Team	Organization
Set clear expectations		•	•	•
Behave accordingly	•			
Avoid telling yourself stories	•			
Embrace accountability	•	•	•	•
Be responsive	•			
Bring the donuts	•			
Talk about yourself	•	•	•	
Cultivate we-ness	•	•	•	
Seek novelty and challenge	•	•	•	
Increase emotional stability	•			
Increase agreeableness	•			
Increase conscientiousness	•			
Increase attachment security	•			

Increase interdependence	You	Relationship	Team	Organization
Increase formal time together	•	•	•	•
Increase informal time together	•	•	•	
Increase amount of headspace you spend thinking about your collaborator	•			
Increase expectations about responsiveness	•	•	•	•
Do more types of things	•	•	•	
Increase task interdependence by establishing reciprocal (or perhaps sequential) workflows		•	•	•
Tighten control of resources			•	•
Create team-level goals			•	•
Track progress toward goals using team-level metrics			•	•
Base rewards on team-level performance			•	•

OVERVIEW OF STRATEGIES

Your task now is to decide at which level—or levels—you would like to focus your relationship improvement efforts.

For example, you may want to start with yourself if you don't have the power, authority, or goodwill to affect change at one of the other levels, or if you want to take ownership of your contribution to existing problems before asking others to get involved.

You may want to start at the level of the relationship with a specific collaborator given the work is ultimately focused on improving the relationship. Then again, there's a chance you're in a bad situation where it would be ill-advised to try to get a collaborator to sit down at the table to solve a connection issue.

You may want to start with a team-based approach given there would otherwise be a risk of you being perceived as going rogue, as disconnecting, or as abdicating your responsibility to the group. That's not good either.

Then again, you may want to start at the organizational level because the issues are so big or entrenched that they are unlikely to budge as a result of smaller-scale efforts.

As you contemplate which level of intervention makes the most sense, keep in mind that you may not fully know how others are feeling. Just because you're in a state of collabor(h)ate doesn't mean they are. People involved in a single collaboration can be at different places in the Matrix. Imagine, for example, you're in the high potential quadrant, ready to increase interdependence. If you're able to single-handedly do so, even as a collaborator is in a state of collabor(h)ate, you could exacerbate their distress. Argh.

If you feel comfortable doing so, talk to your collaborator(s) about how you're feeling vis à vis the collaborative experience. Share any concerns about what you're noticing, as well as any enthusiasms about what you believe to be possible. Heck, tell them you read a fabulous book that has you thinking in new ways about collaboration; do us both a favor and send them a copy. Then, get curious about their experiences. Ask what's working for them. Invite them to complete the assessment to see where they fall within the Mashek Matrix. Ask if there's an appetite to work together to create change in service to enhancing your respective experiences. Ideally, you'd involve as many team members as possible so that everyone's needs and preferences can be heard and so that everyone's ideas can help shape the vision and implementation. Of course, that may not be doable on a large team or even on a small team if a volatile, aggressive person is wreaking havoc on the psychological safety within the team.

After having these talks, decide if you'd like to work with others to create change or if you'd rather start with yourself. Depending on your situation and your organization's leadership structure, now might also be a good time to put on your supervisor's radar that you're undertaking a little experiment to see if you can improve your collaborative experience. Ask for input on your plan, advice, or cautions that may increase your chances of success along the way.

Thus, as is so often the case, no one approach will be right for every situation. Go with your gut on this one.

Before moving on to Step 5, make sure you're clear what level or levels you'd like to explore:

- Just you
- Your relationship with one other collaborator
- The team
- The organization.

Select as many or as few levels as you like. Keep in mind, just because you start your interventions at one level doesn't mean you're stuck there. You can always loop back and try something else later.

Now, grab the set of cards that you had in hand at the end of Step 3. Select those cards that contain your preferred level of intervention in the top right corner: Y = YOU, C = your RELATIONSHIP with one other COLLABORATOR, T = the TEAM, and O = the ORGANIZATION. Set any leftover cards aside.

Step 5: Brainstorm specific ideas

As you saw in Chapters 3 and 4, the theoretical underpinnings of both the relationship quality and interdependence dimensions give rise to a range of strategies on both fronts. The problem, alas, is that these strategies lack the specificity you'll need for implementation.

As I introduced the strategies, I offered several concrete examples along the way of how these strategies might play out in real life.

If, as suggested at the top of Chapter 3, you maintained a list of specific ideas within the various strategies that resonated with you, you'll want to pull that list out now. No worries if you didn't do so; you can loop back any time to capture my ideas. And, more importantly, it's time to capture your ideas.

Here's one approach to doing so. Grab your set of cards and a pile of scratch paper (or, if you prefer, you can use the blank cards at the back of the card sort deck).

Each card that remains in your deck at the end of Step 4 is a strategy for making your desired first move through the matrix and could be implemented at your chosen level or levels of intervention. One by one, look at that strategy. Then, jot down as many specific ideas as you can imagine for bringing that strategy—at your desired level(s)—to life within your local context. Write one idea per piece of scratch paper.

For example, if you're looking to improve relationship quality using the *bring the donuts* strategy as manifest at the individual "you" level, you might generate simple ideas like:

- Literally, bring donuts.
- Clean up the folder structure everyone keeps complaining about.
- Repair the squeaky wheel on Sarah's chair so she will no longer feel sheepish for moving.

Or, if you're looking to increase interdependence at the team level using the *increase formal time* strategy, your list might include:

- Set a second stand up each week.
- Ask for a standing 1:1 with collaborator.
- Ask for a huddle to workshop the report.

Generate as many ideas as you can for each strategy at each level. Try not to edit or evaluate ideas as you go. Be in full-on brainstorming mode. And, fair warning, some strategies are tougher than others to generate ideas for.[66]

It can be helpful to seek input from trusted advisors during this brainstorming phase. And, of course, if you're working toward team-level or organizational-level interventions, engage others persistently and meaningfully every step of the way.

As ideas bubble up, add them to the idea hopper. The goal at this point is to get as many ideas down as possible in response to the questions "What could we do?" and "How might we?" Once you have a stack of ideas generated, move on to Step 6.

Step 6: Systematically evaluate options

Step 6 is all about identifying which intervention ideas generated in Step 5 make sense within your current context.

The best interventions will meet four criteria. They are:

- **Value aligned**. The intervention will be resonant with both the organization's values and your values.
- **Feasible**. The intervention will be doable within the current resource environment.
- **Desirable**. The intervention will be a net positive for those involved (remember the "relationship math" we talked about in Chapter 4).
- **Viable**. You believe the intervention could be implemented despite any political, personnel, or attitudinal barriers that may exist.

With those criteria in mind, grab your stack of intervention ideas.

Remove any ideas that don't resonate with either your organization's values or your personal values (see 6A in the flow chart).

---

[66] I would love to hear your ideas! Feel free to email me at deb@myco. consulting

Those ideas are non-starters. Even if an idea would fly at the organization, you probably wouldn't feel great advocating for that idea if it doesn't also line up with your values (yup, that's yet another reason to join organizations with values that align with your own).

Next, ask three questions about the idea on each of the remaining cards (6B).

Question 1. Would this intervention be FEASIBLE with currently available resources? Using the response scale below to rate each intervention idea (jot your rating directly on the scratch paper):

0	1	2	3	4
Absolutely not	Probably not	I don't know	Probably	Absolutely

Question 2. Would this intervention yield DESIRABLE outcomes for all involved? There are a lot of potential considerations that go into deciding if outcomes would be desirable for all involved. It might be helpful here to reflect on sub-questions such as: Would the intervention improve people's daily experiences, reduce stress, or remove barriers to productive action?, Would the intervention help address needs or interests shared by others?, and What harm might come from this intervention? As you did for Question 1, record your rating, using the same response options as for Question 1.

Question 3. Would the intervention be VIABLE despite any existing political, personnel, or attitudinal barriers that exist? This question gauges whether there are roadblocks that could either derail an intervention's success or create an inordinate lift. While it's important to at least consider barriers, their presence is not necessarily a reason to jettison an otherwise promising idea. Rather, knowing that an idea might encounter pushback informs decisions about how to steer it through the gauntlet.

As you have done for Question 1 and Question 2, record your rating for each idea using the same response scale as before.

Now (6C), look back at the ratings you gave each sticky on each of the three questions above. Remove any cards that received either a 0 on 1 or more qualities. It's not that you can't possibly pursue those ideas, it's just that, as a first pass, it may be advisable to start with an idea that has more going for it out of the gate.

If just a single idea remains, you could opt to iterate back up to Step 5 and do some more brainstorming. Or, you can move on to Step 7 with that single idea in hand.

If multiple ideas remain, sum the three scores you gave to each idea and array those ideas from high to low cumulative score (6D). Do one or two ideas float to the top (6E), perhaps breaking from a cluster of other options lower down the scale? If yes, you're all set. That said, if you end up with a bunch of intervention ideas that all score roughly the same when the three criteria are summed, try tightening constraints (e.g., removing any ideas that scored a 1 or 2 on any of the three criteria) or just selecting a few options that seem most interesting or exciting to you and then move on to Step 7.

If you're feeling uneasy at any point about the number or quality of the ideas you have in hand, here are two options to consider:

- Remember that you can return to brainstorming any time. If you brainstormed alone last time, recruit others to help you out this time. It will be helpful if your thought partners have at least read Chapters 2–4 before pulling up a chair.
- Go back through the three audit questions to see if you used the full range of response options when sorting the intervention ideas. This may help introduce more spread in the summed scores.

If you truly feel none of the intervention ideas can reasonably be placed above the midpoint of the scale, it could be because your workplace truly is unamendable to intervention and change. Or, it could be because you're operating in a fugue of frustration and helplessness that has resulted in you being unable to see the full range of possibilities.

If you're in a dark place emotionally, know it is perfectly normal for your perceptions and thinking to be colored by your emotions. It's not your fault; it's just how the mind works. Recruit a constructive ally who knows enough about your workplace to offer an informed sounding board to help lift you out of the muck. The two of you can go through the card sort activity together. You may be tempted to argue against every positive possibility your ally offers up. Do your best to resist. Try out phrases like, "I'm open to that possibility," "Perhaps," and "Let's play this through for the sake of the thought experiment." You're not actually deciding anything yet. There's nothing on the line. No resources will be wasted by simply imagining if. Try to keep an open stance.

At any rate, by the end of this step, you ideally know which one or two interventions you'd like to activate on first. This doesn't necessarily mean you'll never do the other things; it just means that you know you need to start somewhere, that you know you can't do everything at once, and that you've done the thinking work to tell you where that starting point should be.

Step 7: Plan and implement

I'll keep these next few steps super short, both because you managed to get through the lengthy descriptions of Steps 1–6 and because how you complete Steps 7–9 will depend a lot on your context, your preferred modes of doing, and the complexity of the intervention ideas you're going to pursue. (I mean, let's be real here: If you've decided to literally bring the donuts, implementation is as simple as putting a reminder in your calendar to swing by the donut shop en route to work one day. You got this.)

Step 8: Observe and learn

No one intervention will be the secret sauce that miraculously transforms your experience of a collaborative relationship overnight. Like driving a barge, it's going to take a while to turn the boat around; small adjustments will be needed.

Pause and reflect along the way. Remind yourself what you were trying to do and why (e.g., "I was engaging in deliberate self-disclosure to increase relationship quality with my colleague"). Then ask yourself:

- Did you implement the intervention as intended? If not, why not?
- Did the intervention have the intended effect? How do you know?
- Were there any unintended consequences, positive or negative?
- What have you learned thus far about the effectiveness of this intervention to adjust the relational feature you were working on?

Step 9: Now what?

Have you made the progress you want? Perhaps you've made a little progress increasing relationship quality, but feel there's still important distance to travel there. Great! You may want to give your intervention more time to make an impact, or perhaps you'd like to try and add another idea in the mix. Maybe you've advanced a full quadrant toward your goal. Amazing! Loop back to Step 3 and repeat for the next move along the path (i.e., increasing relationship quality or increasing interdependence).

Reminders and recommendations

A couple reminders and recommendations may be helpful as we wind up this chapter:

Recommendation 1. No one size fits all. Adopt and adapt the model. Give life to its theoretical underpinnings and tactical manifestations however you wish.

Recommendation 2. Don't expect quick fixes. Like all relationships, collaborative relationships develop over time. Persistent, intentional effort over time is the name of the game.

Recommendation 3. Start small. Be curious about the impact small adjustments can have in your collaborative relationships. Rather than try to change everything all at once—a proposition that is at once overwhelming, unlikely to stick, and wastes resources—start small. Observe if and how a little action here begets a reciprocal action there. See if you can build a virtuous cycle of positive change.

Recommendation 4. Think like an experimental researcher. Approach your efforts to enhance your collaborations from the mindset of an experimental researcher. You have a theoretical model in hand. Now, make predictions about the outcomes you expect to see when implementing the various components. Change one thing at a time, then observe the results. Make another tweak. Observe. Iterate. Keep learning.

Recommendation 5. Be transparent. Whether you're an individual contributor, a team lead, or a director on high, say what you mean and mean what you say. While that's generally good advice in any relationship, it's especially important when it comes to collaboration because transparency builds trust. If you're secretive or duplicitous about your goals, intentions, or methods, you will eventually be found out. Your colleagues will feel manipulated. And you'll have a heckuva time earning back their trust.

Recommendation 6. Co-create. Even if you have the authority to do so, I'd caution against acting as the "decider" who uniquely knows what the relationship needs and how to get there. Engage your collaborators in the imagining and implementation. Look for ways to invite others in a meaningful and persistent way. Put their needs and interests on par with your own. Learn from them. Co-create whenever possible.

Recommendation 7. Resist the urge to formalize. Especially if you and your team have been in the unfortunate state of collabor(h)ate for an extended period, any intervention that offers relief or—fingers crossed—a positive trajectory, can feel like an incredible blessing. There can be an impulse to codify the intervention in hopes of holding tight to the progress. Resist. Setting new policies or formalizing practices makes the intervention feel institutional rather than relational, and you want to keep the relationship centered. Plus, if you're in a typical organization, it's rare that outdated or ineffective policies get sunset, which means that, if the future reveals a negative unintended consequence of the intervention, it might have already become entrenched.

Recommendation 8. Commit to maintenance. Without maintenance, relationships degrade. And, in the case of collaboration, if relationship quality degrades, it's easy to drop through the manhole from collaborGREAT to a state of collabor(h)ate.

Recommendation 9. Processes matter, too. Unsurprisingly in a book about collaborative relationships, I have focused exclusively on…well…relationships. This seems just as good a time as any to mention that tools (like technology, touchstone documents, communication plans) and processes are important, too. Check out the Other Links section of www. collaborhate.com for my Collaborative Action Model which lays out a process collaborators can follow when exploring "What could we do?," "What should we do?," "How should we do it?," "Do it," and "How'd we do?"

 # Here's the point

- An understanding of the two relational dimensions that undergird the Mashek Matrix, combined with specific strategies for adjusting each dimension, illuminates a process for moving from where you are to where you want to be.

- To move from a state of collabor(h)ate to a state of collaborGREAT, focus first on decreasing interdependence. Then, increasing relationship quality. Then, deepening interdependence once again.

- Specific intervention ideas may be applied at the individual, relationship, team, or organizational level.

- The workshop described in this chapter provides a flexible and adaptable process for adjusting relationship quality and interdependence.

🄮 Take 5

1. How well did your quantitative scores from the Collaborative Relationship Assessment align with your gut-level intuitions? What wisdom lies in that comparison?

2. Under what circumstances do you imagine you'd be most inclined to preference individual-level interventions? Relationship-level interventions? Team-level interventions? Organization-level interventions?

3. What do you see as the biggest obstacles and opportunities afforded by individual-level interventions? Relationship-level interventions? Team-level interventions Organization-level interventions?

4. What emotions came up for you as you completed the workshop? What felt good or promising here? And, what felt bad or perhaps even doom-filled? Where do you think those emotions are coming from?

5. What do you see as the relative pros and cons of completing this DIY workshop on your own versus in cahoots with your collaborators? What might be gained (or lost) with the different approaches?

Dear Reader,

I hope you're enjoying *Collabor(h)ate* and that you've already encountered ideas to help you and those you work with realize the promise and potential of collaboration.

If you haven't already had a chance to explore www. collaborhate.com, I encourage you to check out the page titled *Perspectives*. This page is loaded with freely available articles, handouts, and other tools that complement and extend ideas from *Collabor(h)ate*. Enjoy!

Next, if you have two minutes, may I ask a small favor? Given how challenging it can be to build healthy collaborative relationships, I'd like to get the ideas from this book out to as many people as possible. Could you help by swinging by your favorite bookseller's website to leave a short review of the book?

Knowing others have found value in the book will help prospective readers decide if they, too, might benefit. Your review may be exactly the nudge someone else needs to take the first step on the path from collabor(h)ate to collaborGREAT.

Ready to talk about the end of
collaborative relationships?
Let's dive into Chapter 6.

Deb

Chapter 6
Getting the heck out

IN CASE IT isn't already obvious: I love collaboration. I love collaborating. And, I love my collaborators. Despite my enthusiastic embrace of collaboration, I'm under no illusion that collaborations are easy or that collaborative relationships should last forever.

Some collaborative relationships are designed at the outset to be time-limited. Others, however, end before the shared goal is achieved. They can deflate, fizzle, wither on the vine, implode, or otherwise go off the rails. When a collaboration goes south or is no longer serving your needs or those of your organization, it may be time to get the heck out of there.

When to get out

Know your off-ramps

One reason people end up in horrendous collaborations is because they ignore the early signals that things aren't going well. They stick around longer than they should, either because they're hopeful things will turn around or because they're conflict avoidant and steer clear of the tough conversations that are needed either to fix the situation or to bring crisp closure to a project.

To prevent these slippery slope scenarios, be explicit up front about what you're committing to; know your off-ramps. For example, if you're exploring co-creating a new product with another company, you could first commit to a series of exploratory conversations. At the end of that phase, you could decide whether you'd like to say "no" or "go" to the full project. The other party, of course, gets to do the same. Like matching in an online dating app, things only move forward if you're both "in", and saying yes to a first date isn't saying yes to moving in together. The key idea here is that you want to be in a collaboration—or any relationship, really—as a matter of choice rather than inertia, force, or otherwise feeling stuck.

> *The key idea here is that you want to be in a collaboration—or any relationship, really—as a matter of choice rather than inertia, force, or otherwise feeling stuck.*

Don't confuse "collaborative" with the "absence of conflict"

Not only is conflict good for business, it is also a key part of your responsibility as a collaborator.

Liane Davey, an organizational psychologist who advises visionary c-suite teams, unpacks the critical role conflict plays in organizations in her book *The good fight*.[67] She makes about a million important points in the book, two of which I'll surface here.

First, if your job entails decision making in service to an organization's interest, you *want* a range of opinions in the room and you

---

[67] Davey, L. (2019). *The good fight: Use productive conflict to get your team and organization back on track.* Page Two Books.

want everyone to be able to put those opinions into tension with each other to identify an optimal path forward.

As one project manager explained, "All we're doing in business is optimizing decisions all day long. How much to charge that customer? What do we do for that customer? How do we respond to that customer? You can't optimize a decision with only one person's input, so you need a lot of different smart people's input to climb the ladder of optimization to get to the right decision. If we want our knowledge workers to optimize decisions, we've got to collaborate."

As one boss told a newcomer to her organization after he neglected to surface his reservations about the new direction of the project team, "We don't pay you to attend meetings; we pay you to have opinions."

Davey likens conflict to everyone holding onto a different edge of a tarp and attempting to place that tarp onto a particular bit of earth during a windstorm. If anyone lets go, the tarp will flap in the wind. If anyone tugs too hard, they'll pull the tarp from others' hands and the tarp will again flap in the wind. If everyone lets go, bye bye tarp. Balanced collaborative tension is the name of the game.

The problem, of course, is that, like with collaboration, few of us are well-schooled in constructive conflict. Instead of holding the proverbial tarp in celebrated tension, we move to silence or violence in the face of conflict.

And this leads to Davey's second key point: failure to address conflict when it kicks up creates conflict debt. Like credit card debt, failure to settle the balance of conflict debt results in a persistent, heavy, and escalating burden that follows individuals, teams, and organizations across time.

Just as not all teams practice productive conflict, not all individuals are equipped for it. Tara West, mediator and co-author of

Self-determination in mediation,[68] points out, "While conflict is a natural (and in many ways desirable) part of any relationship, some people have an easier time working through it than others. When we're able to tune into our feelings, slow down our reactions, and truly listen before responding, things tend to go more smoothly. And while some people will come into a situation with more of these skills than others, all of this can be learned."

What does all this talk of conflict have to do with collaboration? Hold in mind that collaboration is not the absence of conflict, that constructively engaging conflict requires collaboration, and that the presence of conflict is not itself a reason to dissolve a collaboration.

So what are the reasons to get out?

When the relationship math doesn't add up

Interdependence theory, which we first encountered in Chapter 2, has a lot to say about if and when we leave our relationships. While you might reasonably assume that we leave relationships when we are unhappy, the theory predicts otherwise. We don't leave our relationships when we're unhappy; we leave our relationships when we think we'd have better outcomes in another situation.

Let's return for a moment to the relationship math we talked about in Chapter 4. I said that we are all looking to maximize our outcomes and that: Outcomes = Rewards - Costs.

According to this theory, we are happy in our relationships when our outcomes exceed our expectations. Said another way, we are happy when we are getting at least as much from the relationship as we expect we should.

---

[68] Simon, D., & West, T. (2022). *Self-determination in mediation: The art and science of mirrors and lights.* Rowman & Littlefield.

Happiness = Outcomes - Expectations.

And, our relationships are stable (meaning we stick with them) if we believe the outcomes we are experiencing in our current situation exceed the outcomes that would be available to us elsewhere. Said another way, we stay in our relationships unless we believe the grass is greener on the other side. To summarize:

Stability = Outcomes - What you think you could get elsewhere.

These different "equations," which rely on the three variables of outcomes, expectations, and what researchers call the "comparison level of alternatives" mean that relationships can be happy and stable, unhappy yet stable, happy yet unstable, and unhappy and unstable.

Here's the key takeaway, which may feel counterintuitive: we don't leave our collaborative relationships when we're miserable, we leave them when we believe the outcomes we would experience in another situation—another job, on another team, going out on our own as a solopreneur—would be better than what we are experiencing now. It also means that just because you're happy doesn't mean you'll keep that collaboration going for perpetuity—there could be even greener pastures for you to explore.

> *We don't leave our collaborative relationships when we're miserable, we leave them when we believe the outcomes we would experience in another situation—another job, on another team, going out on our own as a solopreneur— would be better than what we are experiencing now.*

When your needs are no longer served

We don't collaborate because it feels good or because it's easy; we collaborate because the anticipated end result clearly relates to the shared purpose and individual interests of the collaborators.

But, let's face it, just because a collaboration initially related to the shared purpose and interests of the participants doesn't mean it necessarily continues to do so. Goals may no longer be shared. Interests may have shifted. The collaboration itself may have morphed.

If your needs—or the needs of your organization—are no longer being served by a collaboration, it may not make sense to continue investing your time, talent, treasure, or other resources in the shared work. Investing effort that does not squarely serve your—or your company's—north star means you'll have fewer resources to deploy in service to more relevant work.

You've got options. Broadly speaking, they are: (a) work with your collaborators to reconfigure the shared work so it once again advances your interests, (b) exit the relationship (gracefully, of course) to free up capacity to invest in work that will more clearly advance your interests, and (c) change your interests. There's no one right approach, but the decision warrants careful thought about what's in the long-term interest of your organization's mission and goals.

When the four horsemen gallop in

John Gottman, a world-renowned relationship therapist and psychological researcher, identified what he calls the "four horsemen of the apocalypse." These are behaviors that, when evidenced in discussions with one's spouse, predict divorce. They are: criticism, contempt, defensiveness, and stonewalling. In his classic book, *The seven principles for making marriage work*,[69] Gottman describes these horsemen as follows:

- **Criticism.** In contrast to complaints, which concern someone violating a specific expectation or agreement, criticisms are global negative assertions about another person.

---

[69] (Gottman & Silver, 1999)

- **Contempt.** Contempt, which can take the form of sarcasm, cynicism, name-calling, eye-rolling, mockery, hostile humor, belligerence, and sneering, signal disrespect and a sense of superiority over the other person.
- **Defensiveness.** Providing reasons or excuses that amount to blaming the other person or otherwise framing your own role as the innocent victim.
- **Stonewalling.** Withdrawing by falling silent, tuning out, and withholding eye contact and other signals of presence.

These behaviors are bad news in any relationship, including your relationships with collaborators. While I'm unaware of any research that uses Gottman's argument-coding procedure to predict team distress and dissolution, I'd bet good money that the presence of these same four horsemen spell doom for collaborations.

If you notice yourself or others in your workplace exhibiting criticism, contempt, defensiveness, or stonewalling, take note: Without prompt and deliberate intervention, these relationships are likely headed for doom, and not just for the people most proximal to the relationship, as one director noted: "Amy was nice enough to me. But she had conflicts with several other people, mostly entry-level people. It became a tenuous situation where I felt this power struggle when there didn't need to be. I just kept her at arm's length, did my job, kept my head down, and kind of moved ahead."

If you notice yourself or others in your workplace exhibiting criticism, contempt, defensiveness, or stonewalling, take note: Without prompt and deliberate intervention, these relationships are likely headed for doom.

When it's clear things won't change

The Serenity Prayer, penned by American theologian Reinhold Neibuhr and embraced by 12-step recovery programs the world over, advises us to accept the things we cannot change, have the courage to change the things we can, and the wisdom to know the difference.

Neibuhr's advice applies to the realm of workplace collaboration. As evidenced by the bulk of this book, I believe it's worth approaching collaborations with care and intentionality, whether trying to establish first foundations or working to repair strained structures. Collaborations, like all relationships, take work.

You may personally be doing all the right things. You may have been more deliberate and persistent in your relationship-building efforts than in any other time of your career. And, yet, the collaboration or your relationships with your collaborators may nevertheless be fraught with struggle and disappointment.

There comes a time when you realize that, even though you have done everything you can reasonably do to get a troubled collaboration back on track, it remains unfulfilling, unproductive, or unsustainable. A colleague may persist in their sabotaging behavior. The team may be unable to walk the walk of their shared expectations. The organization may be unable or unwilling to change in light of feedback. As one HR professional told me, "It doesn't matter a bit if you survey people but then don't do anything with the feedback—it's not enough to conduct a rinse and repeat survey once or twice a year because doing that alone doesn't create change. To create change you must reflect on what people say isn't working and be willing to do things differently going forward."

When the juice is no longer worth the squeeze, accept the things you cannot change.

When the juice is no longer worth the squeeze, accept the things you cannot change.

Then decide what action you'd like to take, realizing that inaction is also an available choice. Depending on your role within your organization and the structure of the collaboration, you could:

- Maintain the status quo/keep trying.
- Move into *bare minimum mode* by doing what you have to do, but no more, saving your energy for more fulfilling efforts.
- Request to be moved to another project with a different team that may be a better fit or better equipped to realize the promise and potential of healthy collaborative relationships.
- Remove a collaborator from the project.
- Leave the collaboration.
- Leave your job.

Again, you've got options. Don't choose a path that amounts to banging your head against that brick wall that exists between collabor(h)ate and collaborGREAT. If one or more of those options listed makes your skin crawl, pay attention to that feeling—it's telling you which paths to decline.

Give credence to your needs and preferences. Shutting these down in deference to others who seem unable or unwilling to exert reciprocal care for the work or the relationship sounds an awful lot like being a doormat. Don't be a doormat. It's not good for the soul, it guarantees the existing dynamic will persist, and it means your ultimate impact on the world will be diminished.

Moving into *bare minimum mode* may sound like a reasonable next step, provided it's time limited. The problem, of course, is others will notice your behavior and will make whatever attributions they like about you as a result. Rare will be the observant colleague who says, "Ah yes, it makes good sense that Deb has moved into self-protection mode by disengaging from the unhealthy dynamic that typifies that team; what a wise self-care strategy." They're more likely to conclude, "Wow, Deb's work and engagement has really degraded; I'm going to need to mention that in her next review. I guess she's not as serious about her career as I had thought."

While the remaining options are more likely to improve your work experience, they are also likely to be more difficult because they require direct action and difficult conversations. I don't propose these options lightly; I know there are risks associated with stepping away or asking others to leave. You may worry about disappointing others, burning bridges, causing turmoil, or being attacked. There's also the issue of sunk costs—you've already invested a lot of time, effort, and other resources into the collaboration; walking away may feel like all those investments have been for naught. I get it.

Here's the thing: It's possible to break up with a collaborator or leave a collaboration in a way that minimizes or eliminates personal and interpersonal risks. The trick is to hold that "relationship math" in mind and to approach the difficult conversation head on and with a commitment to grace. As one advisor told me the day before I fired my first employee, "Do what you need to do for the organization's sake, but do it in the kindest way possible."

> *You can break up with a collaborator or leave a collaboration in a way that minimizes or eliminates these personal and interpersonal risks.*

How to leave a collaboration

If you need to leave a collaboration, or if you need to ask someone to leave a collaboration, the Toolbox below offers seven guidelines for doing so with kindness.

Seven guidelines to follow when breaking up with a collaborator

While there's no one-size-fits-all script for breaking up with a collaborator, these seven guidelines can help you do so in a way that is both direct and kind.

Guideline 1. As much as possible, while still doing what you need to get done, work to minimize the other's costs and maximize their benefits (there's that relationship math again).

Guideline 2. Say what you mean; mean what you say. Be direct. Don't tuck the true meaning of your words behind mushy language.

Guideline 3. Be respectful. It goes without saying, but avoid name-calling, belittling, accusations, eye-rolling, jabbing comments, and so on.

Guideline 4. Have the conversation face-to-face (whether in-person or via video call) rather than via email. Sure, many of us feel more nervous about having a tough conversation face-to-face rather than sending a carefully crafted email. But, because it's so easy to misread what's in the written word and next to impossible to make space for others' reactions, the brave approach is the right approach if the goal is to dissolve the relationship gracefully and in a way that maximizes outcomes.

Guideline 5. Be brief. Say what you need to say in just a minute or two.

Guideline 6. Make space for the other person to say whatever they want to say, though resist engaging in debate, rebuttal, position defending, and so on.

Guideline 7. Behave in a way you'll feel good about both now and in the future when looking back on this moment.

With those guidelines in mind, here's a template of key talking points. Keep your comments brief. Get in. Get out. Get on with it.

- Say what the conversation is about. It's amazing how often this important point is skipped in all sorts of break-up conversations, which leaves the listener asking, "Wait: Are you breaking up with me?" If that's what you're doing, say so.
- Point to the disconnect between your needs (or the needs of your organization) and the realities of the collaboration.
- Say directly what you have decided.
- Affirm your commitment to a graceful transition.
- Propose a follow-up conversation over the next few days to co-create the transition plan.
- Follow up with an email.

The Toolbox below offers a few examples of how to put this template into action: one to leave a collaboration, one to remove a collaborator from a project, one to request a collaborator to step away, and one to request you be moved to another project. Understandably, your situation will constrain which options are available to you.

 Four scripts for breaking up

Script 1. Leaving a collaboration.
"I wanted to tell you personally that my organization has decided to end our participation in the Acme collaboration. As I have shared previously, the focus of the collaboration has shifted such that the needs of my organization are no longer served. At the end of the calendar year, we will no longer commit staff, time, or other resources to this project. I am committed to co-designing with you an off-ramp that is as minimally disruptive as possible for all involved.

I'd like to meet sometime over the next few days to design that process. While we will need to share this news with the rest of the team, I recommend we wait until after our planning meeting to let others know so that we can provide more information about what the transition will look like. I will, of course, follow up with an email to formalize our departure. What questions do you have for me at this point?"

Script 2. Removing a collaborator from a project.
This script is for a hierarchical collaboration where there's actually someone in charge who has the authority to remove collaborators. In some cases, of course, the collaboration is truly co-owned, so you can't just remove someone by fiat. In those cases, the first step of the breakup needs to be a conversation about who should leave. More on that in a moment. First, here's a break-up script a manager or director could use to pull a direct report from a collaboration:

"I have decided to remove you from the Acme collaboration. As I have shared in our previous conversations, relationship quality is a key driver of collaborative success and I have heard from others on that project that you have missed meetings, are disengaged in the meetings you attend, and struggle to complete your action items. These behaviors have hurt the team's ability to make progress on the stated goals. As of today, you are no longer on the Acme team. In an effort to minimize the disruption your departure may have on the team, I will work with you directly to ensure any in-process work you may have on this project is transitioned back to the team. I will follow up with an email to you after our meeting with a list of specific requests, which you will need to complete by the end of the business day tomorrow. I will also send a note to others on the team to alert them to the transition and will ask that they direct any questions or concerns to me. What questions do you have for me at this point?"

Script 3. Exploring the possibility of asking a collaborator to step away.

Now, in the case where a collaborator who co-owns the project is out of step with other collaborators (for example, in the case of three start-up co-founders), a different sort of conversation needs to happen, one that honors the equal partnership and invites a conversation about how best move forward. Here's a script to kick off that conversation:

"I would like to discuss our different visions for this collaboration and decide how best to move forward. In its current state, my (or my organization's) interests are not well served by our shared work. I would like to explore if there's a way to reconfigure the work in a way that truly advances each of our interests or if it would make more sense for one of us to step away from the project. I am committed to an open and frank conversation that holds our respective needs on par. Could we set aside a few hours next week for deep exploration of our options and to see if we can identify a mutually satisfactory solution?"

Step 4. Request to be moved to another project.

Now, if you're an individual contributor who is either unable to make the dramatic move of leaving your job, or disinterested in doing so, it might make sense instead to ask for reassignment. You could say, "I would like to be transitioned from the Acme collaboration. As you know from our past conversations and problem solving, the team is not functioning well. I have worked to improve the situation, but I have been unsuccessful in doing so. My ability to contribute meaningfully to the work has suffered, as have my engagement and job satisfaction. I am committed to co-designing with you an off-ramp that is as minimally disruptive as possible for all involved. I'd like to meet sometime over the next few days to design that process. What do you think?"

Post-dissolution growth

Gary Lewandowski, author of *Stronger than you think*,[70] researches how romantic relationship dissolution impacts individuals. His research shows that individuals are keen to leave relationships that don't provide sufficient opportunity for self-expansion. And, perhaps surprisingly, ending a relationship that provides insufficient self-expansion is associated with an increase in positive emotions and a greater sense of personal growth.

If a collaboration isn't serving your needs, there's a reasonable chance the dissolution of that relationship will afford new growth opportunities for you, your organization, and perhaps even your collaborator.

For example, you might now have time to invest in another promising partnership. Or perhaps you can allocate more resources to another valued project that would benefit from your focused attention. In addition, you can reflect intentionally on the growth experienced because of the relationship.

These are all potential sources of growth from the collaboration that you get to take with you, even when the relationship ends. The trick is to be alert to the possibility of such growth and to be intentional about leveraging it.

All relationships end

And here's a somber thought to close out a heavy chapter: All relationships end. Separate from the collaboration breakups considered above, every single collaboration faces the risk of a collaborator suddenly having to check out from the shared work. Illness, family emergencies, accidents, and death happen. While I don't advise wallowing in dark imaginings, I do think it's

---

[70] Lewandowski, Jr. G. (2021). *Stronger than you think: The 10 blind spots that undermine your relationship…and how to see past them.* Little, Brown Spark.

constructive—and an act of care—to anticipate the possibility that you or a collaborator might one day not show up to work as expected. To minimize the likelihood that a sudden departure would devastate the shared project you believe in, create and use systems that make each person's work readily visible and available to others. For example:

- Use a shared task list or project management tool.
- Maintain a single contact database of fellow collaborators, vendors, and clients.
- Name and organize files in a way that others will be able to make sense of.
- Store those files in a shared folder that others can feasibly access them.

✪ Here's the point

- The presence of conflict is not a reason to dissolve a collaboration; in fact, conflict is an important and valuable aspect of "together work."
- We don't leave collaborations when we are miserable; we leave them when we believe the outcomes we would experience in another situation would be better than what we are experiencing now.
- If your needs are no longer being served by a collaboration, think carefully before continuing to invest your time, talent, treasure, or other resources in the shared work.
- If criticism, contempt, defensiveness, or stonewalling gallop into your collaboration, the relationship may be headed for doom.
- Sometimes, despite having invested a lot of effort to save a collaboration, you come to realize that the collaboration must end; it is possible to do so with grace and tact.
- Personal and professional growth is available after dissolution of a collaborative relationship.

- While none of us likes to think about our or others' mortality, doing so within the context of collaboration means the shared work can carry on, even if a collaborator is unable to do so.

⑤ Take 5

1. What beliefs do you hold concerning conflict, collaboration, and the relationship between the two? How might those beliefs influence your willingness to exit a collaboration?

2. Imagine you're in a collaboration that probably should end, but you stick with it anyway. What do you see as the range of possible downstream outcomes for you, your collaborators, the work, and your company? Which of these outcomes seem most likely? Most desirable? All told, what is the cost of inaction?

3. Think about a negative collaboration you're either in right now or one you were in previously. How might you modify the break-up scripts I provided to make them more appropriate and effective for your situation?

4. Thinking about a collaborative relationship that you have been in in the past, regardless of how it ended, identify at least three ways you grew as a result of that relationship. What did you learn about yourself, the problem you were working to solve, your partners, and/or the process of collaboration? What new skills, perspectives, resources, or identities did the relationship provide? How will you pull these lessons forward into your next opportunity?

5. What steps have you and your collaborators taken to protect your project from being devastated by a collaborator's sudden departure? What additional steps do you think would be worthwhile?

Chapter 7
Hey, you're
collaborGREAT!

L ET'S TAKE A moment to look back at where we've been.

We started the book with the big picture observation that collaboration is both ripe with potential and fraught with frustration. Collaboration is difficult both because relationships are difficult and because desperately few people ever learn how to build healthy collaborative relationships. Unsurprisingly, many people have mixed feelings about this essential enterprise.

In Chapter 2, we explored the Mashek Matrix as a two-dimensional framework for understanding how to move your collaborative relationships from collabor(h)ate to collaborGREAT. Strategies drawn from empirical research in the psychology of relationships (Chapter 3 and Chapter 4) make possible the necessary adjustments. Importantly, the order in which one makes those adjustments depends on one's starting quadrant, a point emphasized in Chapter 5, which offered a DIY workshop on applying ideas from the Matrix to your world.

Chapter 6 made the case that a collaboration "for now" needn't be a collaboration "forever," highlighting that moving on from a collaborative relationship is sometimes the right thing to do.

And that brings us to Chapter 7. This chapter sees you—equipped with new lenses for understanding and enhancing your collaborative relationships at work—standing in front of a wide expanse of possibilities, open doors inviting curiosity and exploration.

As someone who is seen and valued as a strong collaborator, you'll be invited to pass through these open doors. Doors that were previously locked will open. Collaboration will become your key, not just for getting things done, but also for advancing in your career and increasing your agency in the world.

Thus, in Chapter 7 I look at how to choose which opportunities to say yes to, what to consider when you are charged with leading a collaborative project (because you know you will be), and how to leverage your collaborative skills beyond the workplace. Finally, I give some suggestions for moving forward in your collaborative endeavors.

> *Collaboration will become your key, not just for getting things done, but also for advancing in your career and increasing your agency in the world.*

Which opportunities to say yes to

Collaboration is difficult to do well. Because of this, some people avoid collaboration altogether. They may self-select into careers where they don't need to do it, say no to opportunities to join forces, or sabotage shared work, which results in them not getting invited again. In whatever form the "no" takes, saying no to every collaborative opportunity is a bad idea. It undermines one's personal development and job advancement, sure. Perhaps more importantly, it means you can't do much by way of addressing the world's most complicated challenges and realizing the most profound possibilities.

On the other hand, it makes zero sense to say yes to every collaborative opportunity that presents itself. None of us have the bandwidth for that. When we say yes to everything, we're de facto saying no to everything because our efforts will be so diluted and ineffectual as to amount to intentional inaction. And, let's face it: not all collaborative projects are destined for success. It is sometimes possible at the outset to see the bones that scaffold success or the red flags that foretell failure. Add in the fact that none of us are ideal candidates to contribute to every project, and it becomes clear that our involvement isn't always going to be useful for advancing our own interests, much less the greater good. Saying yes to everything is thus just as useless as saying no to everything.

Instead, you want to say yes to the right things. So what are the right things to say yes to? Say yes to opportunities:

- That align with your values, goals, and interests.
- To which you are able to meaningfully and competently contribute.
- That are appropriately scaled for the resources available.
- That involve great collaborators who can meaningfully and competently contribute.

I'll talk more about each of these below, but first, here's the punchline: When any one of those four screening conditions is not met, the opportunity is almost certain to fall short of its promise. Say no.[71]

And, when the stars align and all these criteria shine bright? Say yes. These opportunities are (almost) destined to be collaborGREAT.

---

[71] Or, rather, say no if you happen to be in a position of deciding which collaborations to get involved with. Some of us don't get to exercise such discretion.

Whatever your reason for considering collaboration in the first place, make the *decision* to collaborate just that: a decision. Don't mindlessly slide into collaboration the way romantic couples sometimes slide into marriage just because they have been cohabitating for a couple years and it seems like the obvious next step. Given what's at stake when collaborations go south, be deliberate about saying yes to this important relationship. Once you commit, put in the work to do it well.

Say yes to aligned values and self-interest

Minutes are too precious to invest in work that doesn't align with your values. Spend time on the things that matter to you. That's good advice in life, and good advice in collaboration. It's a slog to sustain effort on work that doesn't align.

Granted, few and far between are the jobs where one gets to wholly self-determine how every minute will be allocated. But, when discretion is afforded, be choosy. Whether evaluating a new opportunity or deciding which existing commitments to scrape from your proverbial plate, reject those that are at odds with who you are and what you value. Say yes to opportunities that align with your values.

Relatedly, say yes to opportunities that align with your interests. People sometimes talk about collaboration as though it's a selfless act; nothing could be farther from the truth.

If your work on a shared project is going to be sustained in a way that truly benefits the greater good, it is essential that you understand how your interests will be served by the work. Some people may be motivated by recognition, others by the promise of a simpler way of doing business, others by having an authentic sense of ownership of the process, and yet others by stipends or other financial incentives.

The chief of staff of a rapid scaling start-up pointed out that incentives ideally stack across multiple levels, too: "collaboration is at once helpful for the community, the company, and to the individual. When you connect collaboration with personal attainment and satisfaction, you're just solving both problems at once."

What motivates you this year may not be what will motivate you a year from now. And different people on the team will be motivated by different interests. As one business consultant told me, "I don't think everybody on the team has to have the same motivation, but we have to figure out for every person what's driving them."

Many different incentives exist, ranging from saving the world to self-development to financial gain. There's no one right way to be motivated. The Toolbox below offers a list of just some of the ways collaborative work can advance individual interests; these are all examples shared by my students, research participants, interviewees, and clients over the years.

Examples of ways collaborative work can meet individual interests

- Become a better communicator.
- Develop a network of contacts.
- Deepen my relationships with others.
- Gain project management experience.
- Get a positive grade or review.
- Secure a job offer or promotion.
- Make a real impact on the world.
- Prove to myself that I can contribute.
- Make use of what I learned previously.
- Create something that doesn't already exist.
- Follow through on a commitment.
- Enable others to do their best work.
- Bring a major effort to completion.
- Gain industry experience.
- Learn about an interesting topic.
- Explore new areas.
- Satisfy my intellectual curiosity.
- Gain experience working on a team.
- Gain professional development.
- Have fun.
- Exercise agency.
- Demonstrate my competence.
- Build my resume.
- Increase my confidence in my own abilities.
- Add value to the project.
- Complete a requirement.
- Acquire knowledge.
- Exercise autonomy.
- Improve an existing product.
- Fulfill a responsibility to others.
- Acquire skills.
- Compete.
- Gain leadership experience.
- Receive recognition.
- Earn more money.

Here are some questions to ask yourself to help determine if, in fact, a new collaborative opportunity might meet this threshold.

- Does this opportunity align with my values, goals, and interests?
- Would completion of this project enable me to advance a specific short-term or long-term goal of mine or my company?
- What about the topic, focus, or nature of this activity interests me most?
- If I were to rank my interest in this opportunity alongside my interests in my existing commitments, where would it fall?
- Dream scenario, how could this project improve the world?
- What's my ideal outcome here?
- What would make all this effort worth it in my eyes?

If an opportunity doesn't align with your values and interests, you could:

- Say no.
- Explore if it might be possible to shape the work in a way that would create the sort of value alignment you would need in order to be "in".
- Change your values. Just kidding. Don't do that.

Say yes to your meaningful contribution

Are you able to meaningfully and competently contribute to the collaboration? By "able," I mean two different things. Both are critically important, and both require some sincere self-reflection.

First, do you possess and have domain over skills and resources that are actually relevant to the proposed collaboration? Your mad balloon animal-making skills might be the perfect contribution to the elementary school fair, but are probably not going to help create a powerful new onboarding experience for hires. Whatever the proposed goals are for the potential collaboration, it's critical that you see a place for you—and your multitude of talents—in the mix.

Second, do you have the bandwidth to contribute to another project? If not, no matter how perfect your amazing skills and talents would be for the project, you'll be utterly unable to contribute them in a meaningful, sustained way that will enhance the shared work. If you're pulled in a thousand directions, you'll end up giving measly crumbs of your attention and ability to the project and to the people you have committed. The project will fall short of its potential. Others will be disappointed. You'll burn bridges. And you'll carry the guilt.

Whether your ability to contribute meaningfully is undermined by expertise or availability, don't agree to collaborations you can't truly contribute to. You're setting yourself up to be the free-rider, and you're setting others up for dashed hopes and unexpected heavy loads as they work to absorb the commitments on which you were unable to deliver.

Here are a couple questions you can ask yourself to help determine if you truly can contribute meaningfully to the proposed work:

- Do you have skills, perspectives, and/or resources that this project needs?
- Are you willing to contribute those things to this project?
- Does anyone else need to sign off on you contributing your time and talents to this effort?
- Do you have the bandwidth to say yes? If not, are you able to clear space for this by removing other commitments from your proverbial plate?
- Is this the right time?

If you will be unable to contribute meaningfully to a collaboration, you could:

- Say no.
- Indicate that you're super interested in the work and would appreciate the opportunity to stay plugged into how the project progresses, but don't make any commitments.
- If you'd really like to be involved in some way, but don't necessarily have the needed skills, make clear what talents and resources you *could* offer and ask if there would be a place for those.
- If you'd really like to be involved in some way, but your limited capacity is the concern, do the hard work of removing commitments from your plate so that you can free up your availability.

Say yes to resources

Without the right resources for the work to be done, frustrations mount.[72] [73] While it is definitely possible for talented people to cobble together resources along the way, collaborations that are reasonably resourced from the outset are more likely to thrive, not least because the people involved can focus their energy on the doing.

Of course, for some collaborations, locating and onboarding the necessary resources is actually part and parcel of the

---

[72] (Knoster et al., 2000)

[73] Knoster et al. offer a framework for thinking about systems change that has likewise proven useful for empowering sustainable collaborative action. They say that successful efforts require five key ingredients: Vision, incentives, skills, resources, and plans. As visualized in the handout provided in the Other Links section of www.collaborhate.com, projects falter in predictable ways when any one of those ingredients is missing.

collaboration itself. For example, if three start-up co-founders are advancing an idea from concept to prototype, one of the co-founders is likely responsible for seeking out and securing funding. So, it's not that all the needed resources must be in place before you would possibly say yes to a collaboration, but that you need to evaluate at the outset whether there's good awareness of what resources will be needed and whether there's a solid plan in place for securing them.

Here are a couple questions to help you make this determination:

- What resources will be needed to launch, sustain, and complete the project?
- Do the others involved have a good sense of what resources will be needed along the way?
- What resources are already available?
- What's the plan for bringing on additional resources as they're needed?
- How much confidence do I have that the people involved will be able to onboard the requisite resources?
- Does the project seem appropriately scoped for the available and likely resources?

If the available resources are nonexistent or insufficient, you could:

- Say no.
- Insist that the project gets re-scoped to align with resources.
- Indicate that you'd be interested in getting involved further down the line once the resources are in place to support this project's success.
- Help figure out how to onboard the necessary resources.

Say yes to good collaborators

The next big question concerns the other people involved: Are they able to contribute in a sustained, competent, and skilled way?

A participant in one of my workshops shared a frustration that I suspect many amazing collaborators face: everyone wanted him on all their special initiatives. He was regularly invited into new relationships and new possibilities to do amazing things—some small, some huge.

Early in his career, he said yes often. And he got burned on more than one occasion. An enthusiastic "all in" start by others would quickly dissipate into oblivion. On at least one occasion, saying yes to the wrong "opportunity" meant having to say no to the right one because there just wasn't enough time in the day to do it all; an opportunity missed. To protect against that same mistake later, he began saying yes even more readily, thinking a few of the projects would fizzle and he'd end up with a balanced slate. Nope. In that case, all the projects clipped along, which meant he was pulled way too thin. The yo-yo of promise, effort, and disappointment drove burnout.

You don't want to miss out on dream opportunities, but you also don't want to commit precious resources—your time, talent, and treasure—to endeavors that are doomed from the start. The other people involved in the project are key to determining whether the project is destined for greatness or "flake-ness" (why yes, I did just make up a word).

If even one of the other key players is inconsistent or incapable, your experience will suffer. Your time will be wasted when they show up to meetings unprepared. You'll be the one working long hours when they fail to complete their action items and thus you absorb the work. Your timeline will take the hit when they create avoidable headwinds by virtue of their exquisite inaction.

> You don't want to miss out on dream opportunities, but you also don't want to commit precious resources—your time, talent, and treasure—to endeavors that are doomed from the start.

So how do you vet prospective collaborators?

Here are examples of questions you can use to pressure test the competence of the prospective collaborators:

- Do the cadre of collaborators collectively have the right skills for the work?
- Will every collaborator bring a needed skill, perspective, or resource to the table?
- If there are skills that will be needed that the collaborators don't already possess, are there plans for how those needed skills will be onboarded?
- Are there people involved who don't need to be?
- Do I have a good relationship with the individuals involved?
- Based on prior experience working with each individual, what do I know about them as conscientious, generous, and competent collaborators?
- What do I know about these individuals by virtue of their reputation?
- When I talk with them about the prospect of working together, what do I notice about their attunement to the complexities of the situation, the realities of their particular circumstance, and the salience of others' interests?

We learn about collaborators' competence over time, as well. A board member of a nonprofit stepped away from her role, despite being passionate about the organization's mission, because others on the board simply weren't upholding their responsibilities as board members. She had personally invested a lot of effort in trying to turn things around, but nobody seemed to care. After a conversation with me about the importance of competent collaborators, she walked, later writing, "Change wasn't happening (or happening enough), so I decided to call it a day. Thank you for being part of the push to quit this board."

If you have concerns about the competence of other collaborators on the project, you could:

- Say no.
- Suggest changes to the composition of the team.
- Share why you have to pass on this opportunity ("This is a tough one for me to pass up given how tightly the work aligns with my values and know-how I have exactly the skill set you need to make this project sparkle. But, having worked with Sam on multiple other projects in the past, I just can't say yes to the inconsistency she brings to the table.")

When you're asked to lead a collaborative effort

People—and relationships among people—are the core of collaborations. When you're collaborGREAT, others take note. Sooner or later, you'll be asked to form the team for a collaborative effort. How do you find and vet collaborative others? How do you nudge the collaborative mindset in others? And how do you create a sturdy container for the diverse perspectives they bring?

Be selectively attractive

In Spring 2019, the Nebraska Tourism Commission launched the state's new campaign to attract visitors. The copy read: "Nebraska. Honestly, it's not for everyone." The campaign was a huge hit, garnering national media attention and fueling pride in the hearts of many of the state's residents, even those of us who have long since moved away from the heartland.

Whether seeking to attract tourists, romantic partners, or collaborators, you really don't need—or want—to appeal to everyone. You want to attract the *right* people.

How do you do that? You flash your firefly booty. Um. What?

During one of my biology courses at Nebraska Wesleyan University, I learned that different species of fireflies flash their little booty lights in different patterns. This allows individuals from the same species to find each other in a field teeming with flashes. When deciding with whom to collaborate, similar signaling unfolds.

Show your beautiful colors out of the gate—who you are, what you value, and how you exist in the world. And, pay attention to what others signal about these same things.

A case in point. I once introduced two colleagues from wildly different spheres—an economist and a brand strategist—because they were flashing the same signals. Whether talking about their values, the visions they hoped to bring forth in the world, the presence of triple bottom line thinking in the way they talked about their work—these two were from the same "species," but were flying in very different fields. They needed to meet.

I introduced them, and shortly thereafter received excited emails from each. They hit it off in a big way, and immediately launched a collaboration that promises to bring about community thriving. One wrote: "Thanks so much for connecting us—it was meant to be! The overlaps were absolutely wild." The other texted: "Talk about a great recommendation…she is one of the most important people I've yet encountered on this journey."

If you're involved in your organization's hiring decisions, it's worth thinking about how to use this idea of being selectively attractive while looking for candidates.

A media editor who once worked in a highly collaborative international news organization said she used to hire for "low ego, high ambition." How did she do this?

Akin to the tourism commission's approach, she was upfront about the organization's values during the very first screening interview. She'd say, "This is a place for people with high ambition, but low ego. If you are the kind of person who is really building your personal brand, I don't begrudge you that. That's great. We should not continue this conversation because you won't be happy here. And we probably wouldn't be happy with you. This place is not for everybody."

Then she'd add, "If you're the kind of person who is about the work itself—you want to do great journalism and you know it's really not about you and you want to collaborate—that's what we do." The right candidates would say, "Thank, God! I've been looking for this."

Screen for a collaborative orientation

Another way of understanding if a person is a good collaborator is to listen to their talk.

During candidate interviews, the editor also listened to how people talked about themselves and their work. If people were highly self-promotional, talking about I—I—I, she noticed. She also noticed if they talked about how the award-winning article was co-developed by a team of reporters, data analysts, and photographers.

A nonprofit leader shared another hiring tip. She said, "I give candidates informal feedback during the interview and see how they react. Or I challenge them a little bit from a place of genuine curiosity. There's no right or wrong answer. I just want to see how they think. And, wow, you can really see how they react live in the moment."

If collaboration is critical to the job or a core organizational value, hire for it. Ask about it. Look for signals that the candidate can walk the walk.[74]

---

[74] I interviewed a firefighter who shared that, to get hired into his department one needs to pass a number of fitness and general aptitude tests, but that collaborative capacity is not something that's screened for until people are on the job. That said, if anyone on the crew does something that puts their colleagues at risk, they're out. As the firefighter told me, "Collaboration is literally a matter of life and death."

Test the waters

In the United States, people generally date someone for a while before committing to a long-term relationship. Dating gives us a chance to experience the other person across a range of contexts, to see how they navigate a range of situations, to see how they respond to our needs, and to see if and how they turn to us in times of need. We learn so much about people just by being with them across time and contexts. It's true of our romantic partners and it is true of collaborators.

If you're positively inclined to collaborate with someone, start small. Rather than launching a multimillion dollar capital project that will unfold over years, perhaps first co-host a two-day conference for industry experts.

Think, too, about the classic prisoner's dilemma game in which two individuals involved together in a heist or other shady dealing are detained. Unable to communicate with each other as they independently undergo police interrogation, each person must decide if they will rat the other person out or hold their tongue. If both people stay close-lipped, the police don't have any evidence for a charge and both people get off scot free. If both people spill the beans, both will get into trouble. And if one person talks, but the other one stays silent, the person who blabbed about the other's guilt will get a reduced charge while the other person takes the heat.

In iterated prisoners' dilemma games, study participants are given a series of tasks in which their behavior—to either cooperate or defect—results in the allotment of points, money, or some other valued outcome. Researchers have explored which of a multitude of strategies results in the biggest wins. The best strategy, which is highly relevant to the advice in this section, is to, first, cooperate in the initial round, and then, in all subsequent rounds, do whatever the other person did in the round just prior.

Thus, in testing the collaborative waters, be an awesome collaborator out of the gate, but keep an eye on what the other person does. If they, too, are an awesome collaborator out of the gate, then follow suit in the next round.

I once had an incredible phone call with a potential collaborator in which we decided to explore offering a new service together. I offered to take a first pass at drafting the statement of purpose, which I did within a few hours of hanging up the phone. I sent the draft right away. When I didn't hear back after a week, I sent a reminder email and also reached out via a second channel. When I didn't hear back after another week, I closed off the possibility of a collaboration. A few weeks later I heard back that the potential collaborator was totally underwater with other commitments. Was I mad? No. While disappointed to not have gotten a chance to work with this amazing person, I hadn't invested a lot of time or energy launching the effort. No harm, no foul.

Observe the other person's behaviors and observe your experience of them. Notice:

- What evidence suggests this person sees and understands your needs and interests? Do they honor agreements around things like deadlines, confidentiality, and contributions?
- Do you see evidence of give and take in terms of ideas, time, processes, and resources?
- Do you feel comfortable sharing half-baked work and is that act of trust met positively?
- What evidence suggests they put your successes on par with their own?
- How do you feel around them?
- Do you sense they have your back?
- Do you feel trusting of the other person or do you find yourself feeling suspicious of their claims?

- How do they receive your efforts to share risks, rewards, resources, and responsibilities?
- Does the other person seem to say what they mean, mean what they say, and follow through on what they say they'll do?
- Are you able to say what you mean and mean what you say when communicating with them?

Nudge the collaborative spirit

Of course, one persistent feature of collaboration is that, well, other humans are involved. And, when us humans are involved in collaborations, they get messy.

Because we need skilled and capable others to be in the mix to keep our collaborations and organizations in the collaborGREAT zone, now is the time to start nudging others in a positive direction. I mean, seriously, can you imagine how incredible collaborations could be the world over if all of us knew more about how to collaborate well?

It is sometimes difficult, at least at first, to see the potential value of collaborative work. But when could-be collaborators enter exploratory conversations with the mindset that collaboration is a waste of time or generally ineffectual, they shut down possibilities and undercut their ability to advance complex strategic goals. You can nudge collaborative mindsets with conversations designed explicitly to open hearts and heads to the possibilities that collaboration affords. The questions in the Toolbox below, some of which have appeared elsewhere in the book, can help. Variations of these questions can be used when contemplating a collaboration among individuals, departments, divisions, or even organizations. You can ask yourself these questions or discuss them with fellow decision makers. Please, adapt them to fit your needs.

10 questions to nudge the collaborative mindset

Question 1. What values does this potential collaborator share with me?

Question 2. In what ways are our respective goals aligned?

Question 3. What's at stake if we do this and it goes smashingly well?

Question 4. What's at stake if we do this and it totally flops?

Question 5. What is the cost of inaction?

Question 6. What is the potential return on investment—not just in terms of finances, but also in terms of organizational capacity, my/our ability to meet my/our most important goals, additional opportunities, and extended networks, both now and in the long-term?

Question 7. What do I stand to learn from this collaborator by working together (e.g., exposure to new perspectives, new skills, sector know-how)?

Question 8. In what ways might a deeper relationship with this person provide value during crises?

Question 9. What about this opportunity feels exciting, resonant, important, or worthwhile?

Question 10. What are my biggest worries or hesitations? This last question can open useful insights about *how* you would need the collaboration to unfold, should it move forward. Separate from if we should collaborate and why, *how* concerns the processes involved in moving from thought to action to create together that which didn't previously exist.

Create a sturdy container for diverse perspectives

Obviously, the people you put on a team need collectively to have the skills and resources necessary to do the work required. This is one of the reasons cross-functional teams are so critical. For example, you want reciprocal learning among product development, sales, and marketing because each of these players bring with them mutually amplifying perspectives, information, know-how, and resources.[75]

That said, these strengths can also present vulnerabilities on the relationship-building front, especially when collaborators inadvertently fill in missing knowledge about others and their work with conjecture, stereotypes, or thin air. When working with people who are different from you in any number of ways—ranging from demographic features to ideological differences to disciplinary lenses—it becomes even more important to invest in knowing the other, decoding your context, and exploring assumptions.

Here are a few strategies for stronger collaborative relationships with others from diverse functional areas, ranks, organizations, generations, geographies, and cultures.

Set the table. When creating collaborative groups, be deliberate about breaking free from entrenched practices around who "should" be at the table. Engage those perspectives that will serve the interests of the project rather than those perspectives that are always at the table despite weak or irrelevant contributions.

As one product manager explained, as a collaborator "you're always going to be at the intersection of different levels of expertise. That means you'll have strengths in some areas and you'll need to balance them out with expertise of others in other areas."

---

[75] Davis, J. (2019). *Create togetherness: Transform sales and marketing to exceed modern buyers' expectations and increase revenue.* JD2 Publishing LLC.

Don't assume you're speaking the same language. Our departments can become overly fond of jargon, acronyms, and code words. As a media founder noted, "The engineers speak a certain language. The product designers and managers have this other language. They have no f*ng idea what each other is saying."

Take the time to explain what you mean when you're using jargon and ask for clarification when you're unsure what the other person is pointing to with their words. Jargon excludes people from understanding what's unfolding in a conversation, as well as prevents them from contributing. The language we use creates ingroups and outgroups. As such, it's important to be intentional about when and why such distinctions serve the interest of the collaboration. Generally speaking, especially when kicking off a new collaboration or when onboarding a new collaborator to an existing collaboration, it's critical to be really effortful in clarifying language that could undermine understanding. Make sure your onboarding documentation includes an LOA. (Wait, you don't know that jargon? Sorry, it stands for List of Acronyms.) Provide a magical decoder ring. Model typing "What is ___?" in the Zoom chat. Make a practice of defining key terminology at the top of presentations.

Be curious about the other's work. I once facilitated a higher ed collaboration that involved a half-dozen universities and a half-dozen functional areas from each institution. There were people around the table who knew nothing of each other as individuals, and who had only a vague sense of what the various titles and roles meant. Faculty liaisons, registrars, transfer specialists, learning designers, academic librarians, associate deans, directors of special projects. Moreover, the same sort of role had different titles at the various organizations and the same titles had different job responsibilities. Add in all the letters behind the names signaling varied credentials. The roster of attendees looked like alphabet soup.

Thankfully, I realized right away that everyone in the room was working with little more than context cues to understand why all these people were in the room together in the first place. We thus started our day with significant introductions: What role does your division play in this project? How do you do your work? What do you value? What are your priorities? What incentives drive the work? What does good work look like? What do you think others don't understand about your division's work?

Seek to understand the other person's/division's interest in this shared project. While you should know what you and your division will gain from engaging in a particular collaboration, it would be a mistake to assume others are likewise driven by the same constellation of concerns or opportunities. Rather than risk the misstep of inadvertently squashing somebody else's valued outcomes, just ask what those are so you can protect them and hold them on par with your own. Ask: What else are you juggling right now and how does this particular project rank? What about this shared piece is most interesting to you? What could we do here that would be particularly meaningful or helpful to you? What do you most want to get out of this experience, either for your division or for you personally? What does success look like for you?

Don't assume that what's appropriate in your local context will be appropriate elsewhere. A global operations manager I interviewed shared a powerful story about the importance of being alert to differences in what's appropriate across contexts. She described how her colleagues from other countries would ask about American politics and politicians, often lobbing a joke or two about dysfunction. Early in her career, she made the mistake of reciprocating the questions and critique, meeting uncomfortable silence and avoided eye contact. Later, a colleague explained that within that country it was risky for people to question the government. The point here is that, whether we're working with colleagues from another country or just another division within our own company, it's important to be a good guest. Spend time researching customs and manners. Ask a colleague to give you a briefing. Ask the point of contact on the other team to offer feedback to support your learning. Offer others on your team cultural onboarding.

Be humble. Intellectual humility is critical in any collaboration, and especially so in collaborations with diverse others. Intellectually humble people know the limits of their own knowledge. Just because you might be familiar with a division's work doesn't mean you know what your colleagues know. Don't tell others how to do their job. Invite others' insights: From your vantage point, what do you see as the opportunities and risks here? Ask to learn: This is an area I know nothing about. What would you say are the key points I need to understand here?

Collaboration in friendships, family, community, and life

Because collaborative relationships permeate every facet of our lives, excellent collaborators deploy their skills in their friendships, families, and communities. Across all these domains, collaborative relationships can either unlock or derail possibilities.

Here are just a few examples:

- The Parent-Teacher Association raises funds to bring a theater program to the school (or, in-fighting results in behaviors that gut the group's ability to get anything done).
- Friends coordinate meal drop off and childcare for another friend who has undergone surgery (or, the friend gets 20 meals one day and zero meals for the rest of the recovery period).
- The Neighborhood Watch partners with the city's parks department to remove a decrepit shed from the park (or,

bureaucratic red tape and the refrain "not my job" creates inordinate barriers to removing the eyesore that currently houses illicit activity).

- Siblings figure out what to do with a parent's belongings after the parent dies (or, tensions rise and emotions explode as people navigate the complexities of grief, loss, and uncertainty).
- Divorced co-parents smoothly coordinate their child's day-to-day life (or, parents weaponize their relationships with the child to hurt each other).
- A landlord and tenant figure out how to pay for and coordinate urgent repairs to an apartment (or, the two move into an adversarial posture of blame).
- Neighbors figure out where the fence line belongs between their properties (or, one neighbor erects a fence while the other neighbor is out of town and causes strife).
- Concerned individuals orchestrate the transport of specific emergency medical supplies to a war-ravaged country (or, a bunch of individuals send whatever they can to an organization they've never heard of and hope it lands in the hands of someone who can use it).
- Family members living under one roof keep the place tidy (or, one person ends up doing all the work, feeling taken advantage of along the way).

This is far from an exhaustive list, of course. What I hope is clear is that collaboration permeates how we live, how we explore, how we relate, and even how we die. In each of these examples, people are working with known others to advance shared goals. In each, cost, complexity, jurisdiction, or uncertainties preclude any one person from going it alone.

If you're so inclined, let's go through one more little thought experiment:

- Jot down all the ways collaboration exists in your nonwork life; record as many examples as you can think of. Some things may be mundane daily tasks (e.g., sharing household chores); others may be uniquely situated by whatever life happens to be throwing at you right now (e.g., hosting an anniversary party for your grandparents).
- Look back over the list you generated. Which single collaboration on this list is the most important or meaningful to you right now?
- Ask yourself: "What's at stake if this collaboration goes swimmingly? And what's at stake if it tanks?"
- Holding in mind a specific collaborator within that collaboration, ask yourself how that one relationship is faring. Thinking back to the Mashek Matrix introduced in Chapter 2, in which quadrant would you say this relationship is right now: collabor(h)ate, emerging, high potential, or collaborGREAT To help yourself situate this relationship within the Matrix, you might answer two big questions: "How good is our relationship?" (relationship quality) and "To what extent do we influence each other's outcomes?" (interdependence).
- Ask yourself: "Does my effort in this relationship reflect how important this collaboration is to me? Do I want to change the dynamics in this relationship? If this relationship is not quite where I want or need it to be, am I ready and willing to invest the effort to improve it"
- Finally, ask yourself: "What can I do about that?"

Yeah, what *can* you do about that?

Flip back to the table presented in Chapter 5, which contained all the different strategies for moving a relationship from collabor(h)ate to collaborGREAT. Recall that these strategies were primarily derived from the empirical research in the psychology of close relationships literature (there were a couple ideas from organizational psychology mixed in along the way).

This means they will port back into your nonwork life with relative ease. These ideas will feel right at home in your parenting, marriage, and friendships. They're relevant to the dynamics unfolding at the co-op, community garden, and place of worship. Indeed, every single one of those strategies could be leveraged within your nonwork collaborative relationships.

Every. Single. One. I invite you to grab hold of these ideas. Make them your own. Bring them to your many relationships, in the workplace and beyond. Your collaborative know-how will create better relationships. Better relationships will create a more connected world. And a more connected world will create more care, curiosity, and creativity.

This incredibly difficult collaboration stuff is so worth the effort.

CollaborGREAT expectations

Participating in deep collaborations amplifies your impact in the world. You will be amazed by how quickly you'll be able to make great things happen when you're engaged in collaborGREAT relationships with high-performing people who know how to play well with others. The next step isn't to race out into the world to do lots of "stuff" for the mere sake of doing stuff. Be choosy. Do the right constellation of stuff to advance your goals, whatever they may be.

Creating great collaborations matters because, well, *you* matter. Your *work* matters. Your *experience* of work matters. Your brilliance, your gifts, your wisdom, your talents, your abilities—collaboration can

> *Creating great collaborations matters because you matter. Your work matters. Your experience of work matters.*

amplify *all* of these in a world brimming with both troubles to be fixed and opportunities to be realized.

Investing in the health of your collaborations and in your own development as a knowledgeable and effective collaborator not only increases your agency to get done what you want to get done, it also helps others do the same. And, together, you all will make great things happen.

You've already taken a meaningful step in your development as a collaborator by spending time working through the ideas in this book. If your path is anything like mine, you will encounter new challenges and snags along the way as you enact the fine art of collaboration with new people across novel contexts and on behalf of emerging problems. But now, with a bit of relationship science in your toolkit, at least your collaborative relationships will no longer be mysterious zones of confusion, tension, and friction.

And, of course, the learning isn't over. For my part, I will continue researching and talking about workplace relationships. If you'd like to follow along or—even better—join the conversation, please know I would be delighted to have you. You will find direct links to my social media accounts and newsletter opt-in in the Other Links section of www.collaborhate.com.

✖ Here's the point

- Say yes to collaborative opportunities that align with your values, goals, and interests; to which you are able to meaningfully and competently contribute; that are appropriately scaled for the resources available; and that involve great collaborators who can meaningfully and competently contribute.
- When pulling together others for a collaborative effort: find and vet collaborative others, nudge the collaborative mindset in others, and create a sturdy container for diverse perspectives.
- Being collaborGREAT pays big dividends in our friendships, families, and communities.
- Continue to invest in your collaborative know-how; doing so will continue to unlock promise and potential, amplifying your impact in the world.

5 Take 5

1. Think about the four screens for deciding which collaborations to say yes to. Which screen do you anticipate will be trickiest for you, perhaps because of your work context, your background, your psychological needs, and so on? Knowing which area might be trickiest for you, what additional screening questions can you offer yourself to help you make timely and informed judgements about the wisdom of saying yes to opportunities?

2. Thinking ahead to the next collaborative effort that you cohere, what ideas from this chapter are you especially eager to put into place for bringing people together and facilitating their collective action?

3. Clarity about your own values, goals, and interests reside at the heart of both the "say yes" decision and the recommendation to broadcast broadly your true colors. To what extent are you crystal clear on your values, goals, and interests? If you don't feel crystal clear, what reflections, conversations with particular others, or experiences do you think would help bring you clarity?

4. What next steps would you like to take in your own professional (or personal) development on the collaboration front? What are three mini steps you would like to take this week to get started on your intended path?

5. What parallels do you see between your collaborative strengths and struggles in your personal and professional lives? What might those parallels suggest regarding important steps in your continued journey?

How to make your organization collaborGREAT

C OULD YOUR ORGANIZATION use a hand addressing the collaborative headwinds that undermine timelines, bottom lines, quality, and morale? Here's how Deb can help:

Books. Purchase copies of *Collabor(h)ate* for your team. The more people in your organization who are thinking constructively about how to build incredible collaborative relationships, the better. Want to bulk-buy copies of this book for your team and colleagues? We can introduce case studies, customize the content, and co-brand *Collabor(h)ate* to suit your business's needs. Please email info@practicalinspiration.com for more details.

Keynotes. As an award-winning teacher celebrated for her wit, presence, and clarity, Deb engages audiences, encourages openness, and motivates action. She provides professional audiences a fresh lens for thinking about and improving their workplace collaborations. Moving seamlessly between data, theory, and practice, Deb drops powerful truth bombs and truth balms about the possibilities and perils of workplace collaboration.

Workshops. Deb's virtual and in-person workshops help people build and sustain healthy and productive collaborative relationships at work. Whether you're looking for theoretical frameworks, assessments, or concrete tools and tips to quickly level up your team's collaboration game, reach out. Participants admire Deb's clear presentations and ability to facilitate productive and stimulating activities and discussions among people who see the world differently (sometimes very differently).

Advising. Whether you're on a new team committed to building strong foundations, on a troubled team that needs to get unstuck, or on a rapidly expanding team that's trying to duct tape together a cardboard car as it hurls down the freeway, Deb helps by providing research-backed strategies and insights culled from multiple sectors.

Learn more at www.debmashek.com and www.myco.consulting.

What Deb's Clients Say

"DEB HAS THE rare skill to present and speak in a captivating way while making it look effortless. Her professional materials are fun, engaging, and easy to follow... If you're in need of a speaker to bring awesome and inspiring energy to your audience or community, Deb is on point. She gets my highest possible recommendation."

"The session had so much energy and most importantly so many items to take back and think about. I highly recommend Deb to anyone whose work involves leading or being part of collaborative work culture."

"Thank you kindly for the time, insight, and infectious energy—such great stuff!"

"The presentation and content were exceptional!"

"Deb would be my absolute first choice for any complex project involving collaboration or facilitation. One of the smartest and most thoughtful people out there!"

"A deep sense of confidence and humility—a paradox of character that is not always apparent in many academics."

"Deb is the ultimate scholar practitioner who 'walks the walk' of collaboration. Count on Deb to clarify and measure outcomes, provide actionable feedback and deliver results while strengthening individual and group capacity. She is exceptional—as a leader, collaborator, and fellow human being."

"I honestly could not imagine working with a more skilled retreat facilitator. Throughout the process, I felt as if she was a member of our department for years; that is how well she understood our history and needs."

"Her presence at the table was incredibly positive and warm and clearly saved us many heartaches and headaches, time, and money. I will not take on new collaborations without advice from Deb."

"She helped [us] understand the levers of change, the way new initiatives could be kindled and sustained in a coordinated, efficient manner."

"Deb's deep familiarity with the…challenges of inter-institutional collaboration enabled her to quickly and accurately diagnose our needs, build rapport with stakeholders, and offer concrete solutions that supported our mission."

"Myco listened intently to our needs, then crafted an engaging, constructive retreat that enabled us to have the conversations we needed most, advancing our goals further than I thought possible in a half-day retreat."

"… Deb is the person every senior leader wants to have on their team and in their corner… She not only takes time to understand each groups' goals but really synthesizes the information in order to forge new pathways that move the needle and accomplish audacious objectives."

"Deb brings a wealth of practical experience to the challenge of assessing opportunities and obstacles to strategic planning, organizational development, and collaborative change management. She is acutely perceptive and outcomes oriented. Deb's pragmatic processes help organizations and institutions catalyze nascent opportunities into actionable outcomes."

Appendix: Overview of the Workplace Collaboration Survey

IN SPRING 2022, I partnered with research consultant and data analyst Dev Crasta to field the Workplace Collaboration Survey via the data collection platform Prolific. 1,100 people employed full-time and residing in the United States participated in the study; 1,092 provided usable data and thus comprise the sample. Key information about the sample appears below.

How many years have you been employed by your current employer?

Range: 0—38

Mean: 7.45

Standard Deviation: 6.74

Age[76]

Range: 25—64

Mean: 38.44

Standard Deviation: 9.80

Gender

Female	50%
Male	50%

Which of these is the highest level of education you have completed?

High school or less	10%
Some college or Associate's degree	13%
4 year degree	48%
Post graduate degree	29%

Sector

Accommodation and Food Services	3%
Administrative and Support and Waste Management and Remediation Services	<1%
Agriculture, Forestry, Fishing and Hunting	<1%
Arts, Entertainment, and Recreation	5%
Construction	2%
Educational Services	15%
Finance and Insurance	9%

---

[76] Age, gender, and education data were collected by Prolific and shared with the consent of each respondent.

Health Care and Social Assistance	13%
Information	6%
Management of Companies and Enterprises	1%
Manufacturing	7%
Mining, Quarrying, and Oil and Gas Extraction	<1%
Other Services (except Public Administration)	6%
Professional, Scientific, and Technical Services	14%
Public Administration	4%
Real Estate and Rental and Leasing	1%
Retail Trade	7%
Transportation and Warehousing	3%
Utilities	2%
Wholesale Trade	2%

Which of the following best describes your company or organization?

Government	15%
Nonprofit	15%
Privately owned, for profit	55%
Publicly owned, for profit	15%

How many people does your company or organization employ?

1–99	23%
100–499	22%
500–999	13%
1,000–4,999	13%
5,000–9,999	9%
10,000 or more	20%

Which of the following most closely describes your current level within your organization?

Entry-level	14%
Intermediate or experienced (senior staff)	36%
First-level management	17%
Middle management	24%
Senior management	6%
Executive management	3%

With gratitude

I AM STRUGGLING mightily to find the right words to capture how moved I have been at every single turn of this book-writing adventure by the generosity and support of complete strangers, trusted colleagues, and treasured friends.

Thankful. Touched. Honored. These words are all true, but they somehow feel too small, too psychologically light.

Held. Loved. Nourished. Made whole. Yeah, that's more like it.

To every single person who contributed data, expertise, feedback, perspectives, questions, encouragement, support, resources, sounding boards, and needed distractions: thank you for being collaborGREAT. Seriously, just thinking about your kindness brings goosebumps to my arms, tears to my eyes, and warmth to my heart.

Thank you to the 1,100 individuals who shared their perspectives via the Workplace Collaboration Survey.

Thank you to the hundreds of scholars who conducted the painstaking research that informed the recommendations offered in this book; you've been part of my journey longer than most.

Thank you to my wonderful LinkedIn community for sharing your perspectives on my half-baked ideas. You shined needed light on ideas worth developing.

Thank you to my clients for trusting me with the hardest parts and for inviting me in to work alongside you to create solutions.

Thank you to my collaborators far and wide, past and present. I know what I know about how to collaborate because of you. Your wisdom and know-how are evidenced on every page of this book. My faith in collaboration is due in no small part to what we were able to achieve together.

Thank you to those who graciously spent time with me noodling over why we collabor(h)ate and what it takes to be collaborGREAT, including: Charlie Anastasi, Ted Barnett, JJ Berney, Michelle Berney, Mike Chlanda, Kyle Emile, Jason Fearnow, Debi Ghate, Terren Klein, Rivka Little, Manon Loustaunau, Jacqueline Pfeffer Merrill, Mary Moseley, Holly Ojalvo, Jason Ojalvo, Brian Oulton, Tim Powers, Lisa J. Richer, Paul Roossin, Susan Vetrano, Aleina Wachtel, Annafi Wahed, Bennet Zelner, and others.

Thank you to the researchers and practitioners who served as sounding boards along the way. Your thinking sharpened mine. Kari Anderson, Eric Brooker, Orin Davis, Sean Everett, Keith Ferrazzi, Adam Grant, Zac McClure, Cathy Nylin, Talli Pinhasi, Gene Rendino, Emily Smith, Jodie Steele, Jennifer Newbill, Jennifer Tomlinson, James Tyer, Xiaomeng (Mona) Xu, and others.

Thank you to the kind souls who joined me in The Collaboratorium in the early months to workshop ideas, celebrate baby steps, and jump in with support. This book is better because of you. Jon Adler, Karina Anderson, Joshua Aronson, Helen Beedham, JJ Berney, Esther Bukai, Tiffany Berry, Joy Burnford, Gary P. Chimes, Mike Chlanda, Sandy Shaneyfelt Connolly, Richanah Daly, Richard Davies, Orin Davis, Aissatou Diouck, Sarah Douville, Pat Dunne, Jonathan

Dunnett, Lesley Evans, Stacei Farritor-Hunt, Kelliann Schrage Flores, Susan Haigh, Shira Harary, Yonit Harary, Hilary Jacobs, Sarah Hauser, Clare Kumar, Wei-Ming Lam, Jenny Lambe, Rivka Little, Diana Milillo-Portugal, Patricia Eszter Margit, Juliette Melton, Jacqueline Pfeffer Merrill, Heather Holbert Murphy, Katherine Maloney Pham, Krista Powell Edwards, Penny Pullan, Claire O'Hanlon, Holly Ojalvo, Claire Ramsbottom, Dianna Renz, Lisa J. Richer, Fernando Senior, Alice Sheldon, Asya Spears, Jodie Steele, Michelle Steiner, Martha Mohr Stuewig, Christian Valerio, Deborah Vinal, Aleina Wachtel, Rikki Walters, Tonya Warneke, Tara West, Karen Williamson, Meg Worley, Xiaomeng (Mona) Xu, and Dawn Zerbs.

Thank you to my formal and informal advisors who reminded me what questions needed asking, showed me the trail heads, and guided the journey. I slept better because of you. Baruch Bebchick, Kara Boyer, Esther Bukai, JC Carlson, Susan Chamberlin, Liane Davey, Shira Dicker, Nina Delmonaco, Bruce Gray, Tammy Heermann, Matt Hutson, Joe Kolman, Julie Livingston, Brian Oulton, Allen King, Hannah King, Juliette Melton, Michael Nanfi to, Deborah Obendorf, Elaine Palucki, Kristina Powers, Cindy Skalicky, Lenore Skenazy, and Jon Zimmerman.

Thank you to Alison Jones and the incredible team at Practical Inspiration Publishing. People told me that writing a book would be a lonely endeavor. My experience has been anything but because of you. Your expertise, care, conscientiousness, coaching, and community made writing a book way more fun—and way more navigable—than I could have ever imagined. I am proud of what we have created together. Thank you, too, to all the regulars around the Friday Campfire for sharing know-how, insight, vulnerability, and encouragement on the weekly. I treasure you.

Thank you to Dev Crasta for lending your brilliance to the design, implementation, and analysis of the Workplace Collaboration

Survey. I stand in awe of your know-how, patience, and grace. The fact you did all this while also bouncing a baby in your arms, wrangling a toddler, and holding down your real job proves you and Beka know a thing or two about collaboration.

Thank you to Amy Trinh for lending your design know-how to every inch of both this book and my business. You originated the ideas for the cover, created the images on these pages, and somehow managed to organize my scattered aspirations into gorgeous websites and coherent outreach. It has been such a delight to work with you over the past two years.

Thank you to Helen Beedham, Ron Riggio, and Tara West for volunteering to read an early draft. I stand in unending gratitude for the generous, thorough, and actionable feedback you provided on every single stitch of the manuscript.

Thank you to Carolyn Hiler for supporting my learning, growing, and becoming.

Thank you to all my friends who held space for the anxieties and the celebrations, sent encouraging texts, brought wine, and reminded me to leave the house to play bridge, play with clay, and chase dragonflies. I made it to the other side of this book as a better me because of you.

Thank you to Gerry Ohrstrom for being a treasured base of comfort, adventure, and friendship. You believed enough in me and my ideas to invest in this project; that means more to me than I can possibly express.

Finally, thank you to my son, Rocco, for being my butler on those days when I was head-down for hours on end working on *Collabor(h)ate*. You kept me well-fed, well-hydrated, and fully caffeinated. Your great questions, sage advice, and clever suggestions along the way enriched my experience as both an author and a mom. Your kindness, wisdom, and curiosity never cease to amaze me.

As much as this book offers a cautionary tale about the challenges of collaboration, you all are a testament to the possibilities. When smart, generous, fun people join forces, amazing things happen.

With a heart full of gratitude,

Deb

Index

Printed in the USA
CPSIA information can be obtained
at www.ICGtesting.com
LVHW081746031123
762986LV00046B/1052

9 781788 603829